# BLACK CANYON OF THE GUNNISON NATIONAL PARK ACTIVITY BOOK

## PUZZLES, MAZES, GAMES, AND MORE ABOUT BLACK CANYON OF THE GUNNISON NATIONAL PARK

**NATIONAL PARKS ACTIVITIES SERIES**

# BLACK CANYON OF THE GUNNISON NATIONAL PARK ACTIVITY BOOK

Copyright 2022
Published by Little Bison Press

The author acknowledges that the land on which Black Canyon of the Gunnison National Park is located are the traditional lands of Núu-agha-tʉvʉ-pʉ (Ute) Tribe.

**LITTLE BISON**

Press

For more free national parks activities, visit
www.littlebisonpress.com

# About Black Canyon of the Gunnison

Black Canyon of the Gunnison National Park is located in the state of Colorado. The park gets its name from the canyon's steep inner walls, often shrouded in shadows, making them appear black.

The park is famous for its incredibly narrow canyon, which was carved over millions of years by the Gunnison River. Cutting through 1.7 billion-year-old Precambrian metamorphic rock, the park is home to some of the oldest exposed rock in the world. This inner canyon is rugged. If you get a permit to hike in, visitors must be prepared to face tough conditions and remote terrain.

Just outside the park, visitors can also explore the East Portal. This area is a popular haven for fishing and offers an opportunity to peer up at the Black Canyon from within its depths. East Portal was named after a small town that used to exist on the slopes of the canyon. In the early 1900s, the residents of this town worked to dig a tunnel to direct water from the river to fields in the west to water crops.

Black Canyon of the Gunnison National Park is famous for:
- extreme kayaking conditions
- difficult hikes
- rock scrambles

Hey, I'm Parker!

I'm the only snail in history to visit every National Park in the United States! Come join me on my adventures in Black Canyon of the Gunnison National Park.

Throughout this book, we will learn about the history of the park, the animals and plants that live here, and things to do if you ever visit in person. This book is also full of games and activities!

Last but not least, I am hidden 9 times on different pages. See how many times you can find me. This page doesn't count!

# Black Canyon of the Gunnison Bingo

Let's play bingo! Cross off each box you are able to during your visit to the national park. Try to get a bingo down, across, or diagonally. If you can't visit the park, use the bingo board to plan your perfect trip.

Pick out some activities you would want to do during your visit. What would you do first? How long would you spend there? What animals would you try to see?

| SPOT A SALAMANDER | SEE THE CANYON | GO FOR A HIKE | TAKE A PICTURE AT AN OVERLOOK | WATCH A MOVIE AT THE VISITORS CENTER |
| --- | --- | --- | --- | --- |
| IDENTIFY A TREE | LEARN ABOUT THE INDIGENOUS PEOPLE WHO LIVE IN THIS AREA | WITNESS A SUNRISE OR SUNSET | OBSERVE THE NIGHT SKIES | GO SNOWSHOEING |
| HEAR A BIRD CALL | SPOT A WINDING RIVER | FREE SPACE | LEARN ABOUT THE ASTRONOMY FESTIVAL | SPOT SOME ANIMAL TRACKS |
| PICK UP TEN PIECES OF TRASH | HAVE A PICNIC | SEE A MULE DEER | GO FOR A SCENIC DRIVE | SPOT A BIRD OF PREY |
| LEARN ABOUT THE GEOLOGY OF BLACK CANYON | SEE SOMEONE RIDING A HORSE | GO CAMPING | VISIT A RANGER STATION | PARTICIPATE IN A RANGER-LED ACTIVITY |

# Black Canyon of the Gunnison National Park

Date: _____

Season: _____

Who I went with: _____

Which entrance: _____

How was your experience? Write a few sentences about your trip. Where did you stay? What did you do? What was your favorite activity? If you haven't visited the park yet, write a paragraph pretending that you did.

_____

_____

_____

_____

_____

## STAMPS

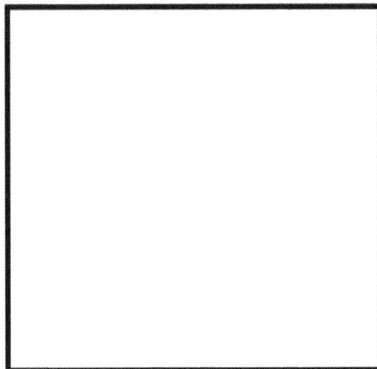

Many national parks and monuments have cancellation stamps for visitors to use. These rubber stamps record the date and location that you visited. Many people collect the markings as a free souvenir. Check with a ranger to see where you can find a stamp during your visit. If you aren't able to find one, you can draw your own.

# Take a Hike

Go for a hike with your friends or family. If you aren't able to visit Black Canyon of the Gunnison National Park, go for a walk in a park near where you live. Read through the prompts before your walk and finish the activities after you return.

Draw something you saw that moves:

Draw something you saw when you looked up:

Draw something you saw that grows out of the ground:

Draw a picture of your favorite part of the walk:

# Color the Canyon

The rock walls of the canyon are steep.
Color the Black Canyon with the river running through the middle.

# Go Horseback Riding on the Deadhorse Trail

Help find the horse's lost shoe!

start here →

**DID YOU KNOW?**

Horseback riding is a popular activity here. On this trail, you can go on day trips. Riders should be sure to bring a first aid kit for themselves as well as their horses.

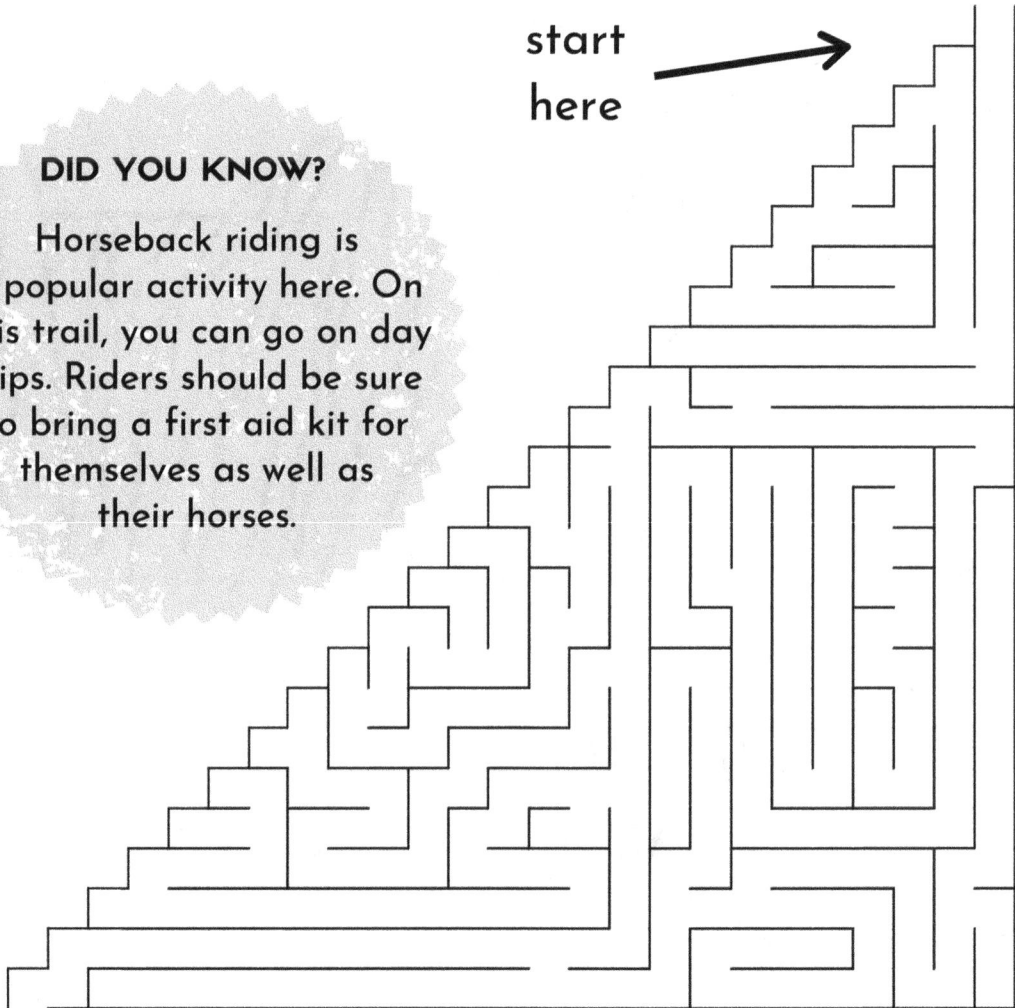

# Hidden Picture

This is one of the most important safety items used by the adventurers on the Gunnison River.

| | | | | | | | | | | | |
|---|---|---|---|---|---|---|---|---|---|---|---|
| 5 | 5 | 5 | 5 | 5 | 5 | 5 | 5 | 5 | 5 | 5 | 5 |
| 5 | 5 | 1 | 1 | 5 / 1 | 5 | 5 | 5 / 1 | 1 | 1 | 5 | 5 |
| 5 | 5 | 1 | 1 | 1 | 5 / 3 | 5 / 3 | 1 | 1 | 1 | 5 | 5 |
| 5 | 5 | 2 | 2 | 2 | 3 | 3 | 2 | 2 | 2 | 5 | 5 |
| 5 | 5 | 2 | 2 | 2 | 3 / 2 | 3 / 2 | 2 | 2 | 2 | 5 | 5 |
| 5 | 5 / 1 | 1 | 1 | 1 | 1 | 1 | 1 | 1 | 1 | 5 / 1 | 5 |
| 5 | 1 | 1 | 1 / 3 | 1 | 1 | 1 | 1 | 1 / 3 | 1 | 1 | 5 |
| 5 | 3 | 3 | 3 | 3 | 4 | 4 | 3 | 3 | 3 | 3 | 5 |
| 5 | 1 | 1 | 3 / 1 / 3 | 1 | 1 | 1 | 1 | 3 / 1 / 3 | 1 | 1 | 5 |
| 5 | 3 | 3 | 3 | 3 | 4 | 4 | 3 | 3 | 3 | 3 | 5 |
| 5 | 1 | 1 | 3 / 1 | 1 | 1 | 1 | 1 | 3 / 1 | 1 | 1 | 5 |
| 5 | 1 | 1 | 1 | 1 | 1 | 1 | 1 | 1 | 1 | 1 | 5 |

### Directions:

You will need crayons or colored pencils in each of the listed colors. Use the color code to help you figure out what the hidden picture is. For example, you will color every square with the number 5 light blue. Some squares will call for more than one color.

1-Orange
2-Yellow
3-Black
4-Gray
5-Light Blue

9

# Exploring the Dark Sky

This park is a popular destination for stargazing. You may see stars in the night sky here that you may not see at home. Why do you think that is?

For all of time, people from across the world have looked at the night sky and seen images in the stars. They created stories about groups of stars, also called constellations. Create your own constellation that you see in the starfield below!

What is your constellation named?

# Where is the Park?

Black Canyon of the Gunnison National Park is in the Rocky Mountain region of the United States. It is located in Colorado. This state is home to three other national parks: Rocky Mountain, Mesa Verde, and Great Sand Dunes.

Wyoming

## Colorado

Look at the shape of Colorado. Can you find it on the map? Don't mistake it for the state of Wyoming, which is similarly shaped!

If you are from the US, can you find your home state? Color Colorado red. Put a star on the map where you live.

# Connect the Dots #1

Connect the dots to figure out what this tiny critter is. There are four types of these that live in Black Canyon of the Gunnison National Park.

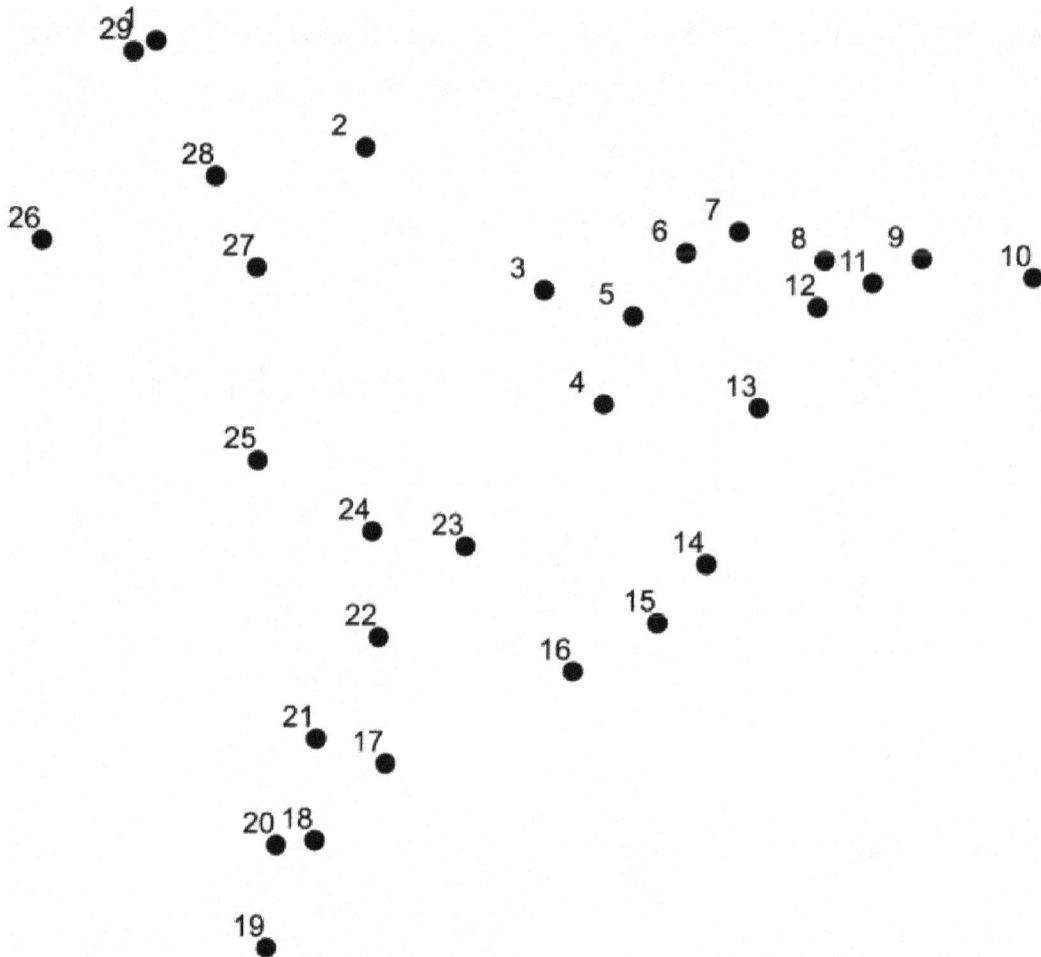

29 1
2
28
26
27
6 7
3 8 9
5 11 10
12
4 13
25
24 23
14
22 15
16
21 17
20 18
19

Their heart rate can reach as high as 1,260 beats per minute and a breathing rate of 250 breaths per minute. Have you ever measured your breathing rate? Ask a friend or family member to set a timer for 60 seconds. Once they say "go," try to breathe normally. Count each breath until they say "stop." How do your breaths per minute compare to hummingbirds?

_____

_____

# Design a Set of Stickers

Imagine you have been hired to design a sticker set that will be for sale in the national park gift shop. These stickers will be a souvenir for visitors to put on water bottles, notebooks, laptops, and more.

You could include a plant or animal that lives here, the park name and the year it was established, or a famous place in the park or activity that you can do while visiting. Make sure to use colors that you think represent the park!

# Who Lives Here?

Below are 8 plants and animals that live in the park.
Use the word bank to fill in the clues below.

WORD BANK: MILKSNAKE, DOUGLAS FIR, UTAH JUNIPER, MERLIN, RINGTAIL, CHUKAR, MINK, OSPREY

☐☐☐ G ☐☐☐☐

☐☐ U ☐☐☐

☐☐☐☐ N

☐☐☐☐ ■ ☐ N ☐☐☐☐

☐ I ☐☐

☐☐☐☐☐ S ■ ☐☐☐

O ☐☐☐☐☐

☐☐☐☐ N ☐☐

# Animals of Black Canyon of the Gunnison National Park

**Beavers**
are the largest North American rodent.

**Porcupines**
are well known for their defense mechanism, their quills.

**Chukars**
walk, run and hop more than they fly.

**Minks**
can swim up to 100 feet underwater and jump from tree to tree.

**Ospreys**
are excellent fishers.

# Common Names
## vs.
# Scientific Names

A common name of an organism is a name that is based on everyday language. You have heard the common names of plants, animals, and other living things on tv, in books, and at school. Common names can also be referred to as "English" names, popular names, or farmer's names. Common names can vary from place to place. The word for a particular tree may be one thing, but that same tree has a different name in another country. Common names can even vary from region to region, even in the same country.

Scientific names, or Latin names, are given to organisms to make it possible to have uniform names for the same species. Scientific names are in Latin. You may have heard plants or animals referred to by their scientific name or parts of their scientific names. Latin names are also called "binomial nomenclature," which refers to a two-part naming system. The first part of the name - the generic name - refers to the genus to which the species belongs. The second part of the name, the specific name, identifies the species. For example, Tyrannosaurus rex is an example of a widely known scientific name.

**American Black Bear**

Ursus americanus

COMMON NAME

**Elk**

Cervus canadensis

## LATIN NAME = GENUS + SPECIES

Elk = Cervus canadensis

Black Bear = Ursus americanus

# Find the Match!
# Common Names and Latin Names

Match the common name to the scientific name for each animal. The first one is done for you. Use clues on the page before and after this one to complete the matches.

| | |
|---|---|
| Elk | Haliaeetus leucocephalus |
| Silky Lupine | Ursus americanus |
| Two-needle Pinyon | Accipiter cooperii |
| American Black Bear | Ochotona princeps |
| Great Horned Owl | Lupinus sericeus |
| Bald Eagle | Pituophis catenifer |
| Coopers's Hawk | Bubo virginianus |
| Pika | Cervus canadensis |
| Gophersnake | Pinus edulis |

**Bald Eagle**

Haliaeetus leucocephalus

Cooper's Hawk
Accipiter cooperii

Two-Needle Pinyon
Pinus edulis

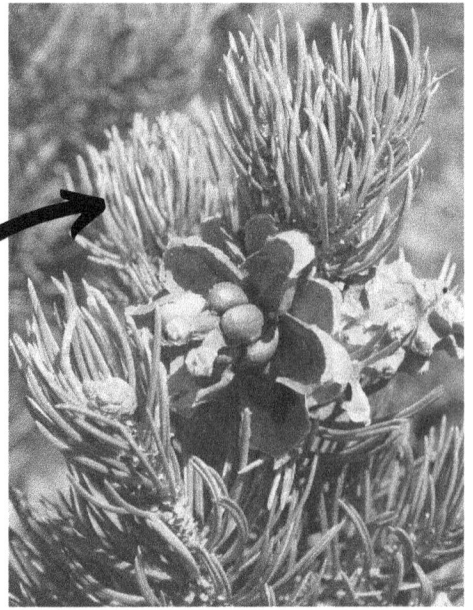

Great Horned Owl
Bubo virginianus

## Some plants and animals that live at Black Canyon

Silky Lupine
Lupinus sericeus

Pika
Ochotona princeps

Gophersnake
Pituophis catenifer

# Things To Do Jumble

Unscramble the letters to uncover activities you can do while in Black Canyon of the Gunnison National Park. Hint: each one ends in -ing.

1. IHFS
   ☐☐☐☐ING

2. IHK
   ☐☐☐ING

3. DBIR
   ☐☐☐☐ING

4. MACP
   ☐☐☐☐ING

5. KINICPC
   ☐☐☐☐☐☐☐ING

6. EISSTEHG
   ☐☐☐☐☐☐☐☐ING

7. SARTGZA
   ☐☐☐☐☐☐☐ING

## Word Bank

birding
reading
camping
stargazing
horseback riding
hiking
scrambling
singing
fishing
sightseeing
picnicking

# Latitude and Longitude

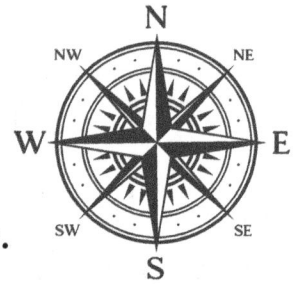

## Plot the points and reveal the hidden picture.

Latitude and longitude is a grid system across the surface of Earth that allows people to locate an exact place. **Latitude** marks how far north or south of the Equator (zero degrees) a spot is. **Longitude** determines how far east or west a spot is from the prime meridian (zero degrees). Using latitude and longitude coordinates, you can pinpoint positions accurately.

If you need help remembering the difference between longitude and latitude, try this!

Latitude lines look flat, stretching around the middle of the globe horizontally.

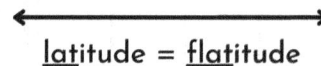

latitude = flatitude

Plot these coordinates on the latitude and longitude using the grid on the right. Place a dot at each coordinate. Go in order plotting one coordinate at a time, and draw a line connecting each dot as you go. Aim for the center of each dot when drawing lines to create the best picture. When a coordinate says "STOP" after it, you should end the lines there. Start a new line between the next set of coordinates when instructed.

1. 30°S, 7°W (START)
2. 43°S, 7°W
3. 43°S, 7°E
4. 30°S, 7°E
5. 30°S, 7°W (STOP)
6. 40°N, 0° (START)
7. 0°, 24°E
8. 0°, 16°E
9. 15°S, 24°E
10. 15°S, 16°E
11. 30°S, 24°E
12. 30°S, 24°W
13. 15°S, 16°W
14. 15°S, 24°W
15. 0°, 16°W
16. 0°, 24°W
17. 40°N, 0° (STOP)

# Plotting Latitude and Longitude

Use the directions on the left page and plot each point listed.

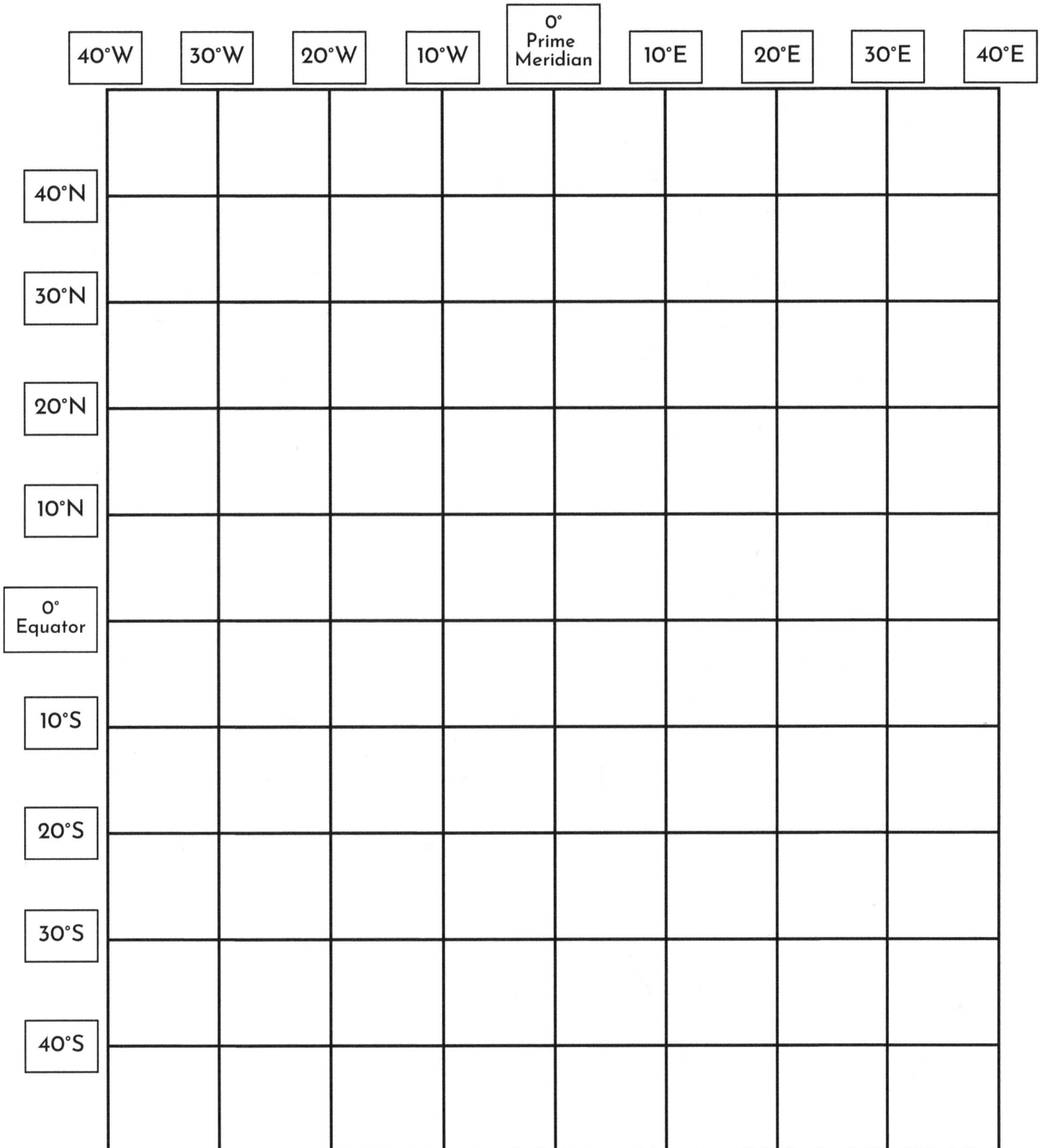

| | 40°W | 30°W | 20°W | 10°W | 0° Prime Meridian | 10°E | 20°E | 30°E | 40°E |
|---|---|---|---|---|---|---|---|---|---|
| 40°N | | | | | | | | | |
| 30°N | | | | | | | | | |
| 20°N | | | | | | | | | |
| 10°N | | | | | | | | | |
| 0° Equator | | | | | | | | | |
| 10°S | | | | | | | | | |
| 20°S | | | | | | | | | |
| 30°S | | | | | | | | | |
| 40°S | | | | | | | | | |

21

# The National Park Logo

The National Park System has over 400 units in the US. Just like Black Canyon of the Gunnison National Park, each location is unique or special in some way. The areas include other national parks, historic sites, monuments, seashores, and other recreation areas.

Each element of the National Park emblem represents something that the National Park Service protects. Fill in each blank below to show what each symbol represents.

```
WORD BANK:
MOUNTAINS, ARROWHEAD, BISON,
SEQUOIA TREE, WATER
```

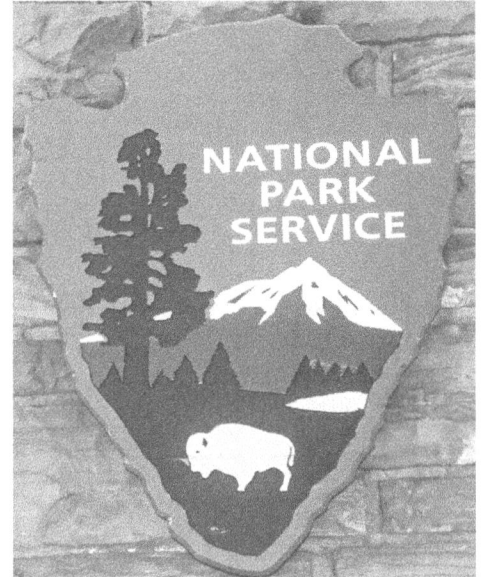

This represents all plants: _____

This represents all animals: _____

This represents the landscapes: _____

This represents the waters protected by the park service: _____

This represents the historical and archeological values: _____

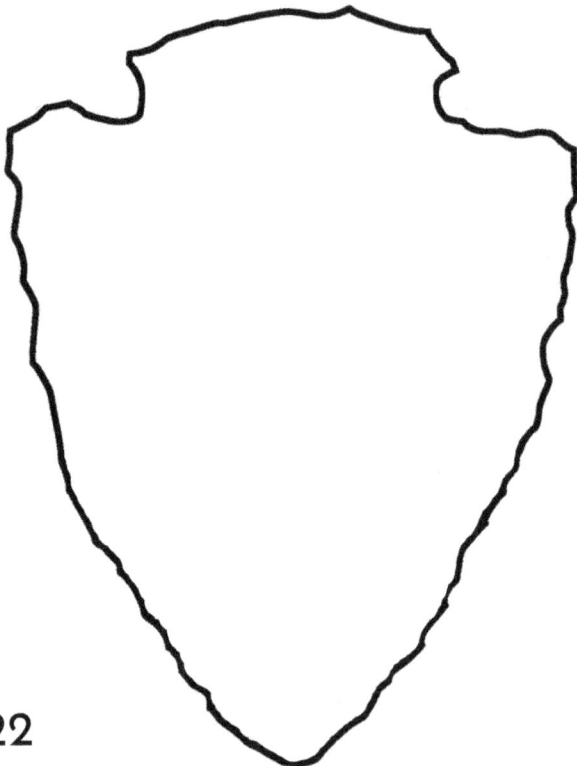

Now it's your turn! Pretend you are designing a new national park. Add elements to the design that represent the things your park protects.

What is the name of your park?

Describe why you included the symbols that you chose. What do they mean?

# The Ten Essentials

Careful preparation and knowledge are key to a successful adventure into Black Canyon of the Gunnison's backcountry.

The ten essentials are a list of things that are important to have when you go for longer hikes. If you go on a hike in the <u>backcountry</u>, it is especially important that you have everything you need in case of an emergency. If you get lost or something unforeseen happens, it is good to be prepared to survive until help finds you.

The ten essentials list was developed in the 1930s by an outdoors group called the Mountaineers. Over time and technological advancements, this list has evolved. Can you identify all the things on the current list? Circle each of the "essentials" and cross out everything that doesn't make the cut.

| | | | | |
|---|---|---|---|---|
| fire: matches, lighter, tinder, and/or stove | a pint of milk | extra money | headlamp, plus extra batteries | extra clothes |
| extra water | a dog | Polaroid camera | bug net | lightweight games, like a deck of cards |
| extra food | a roll of duct tape | shelter | sun protection, such as sunglasses, sun-protective clothes, and sunscreen | knife, plus a gear repair kit |
| a mirror | navigation: map, compass, altimeter, GPS device, or satellite messenger | first aid kit | extra flip-flops | entertainment, such as video games or books |

**Backcountry** - a remote, undeveloped rural area.

# Connect the Dots #2

This animal lives in almost every state in the US, including Black Canyon of the Gunnison National Park. They are nocturnal, more active at night, and sleep during the day. They are omnivorous eaters, meaning they eat both plants and animals.

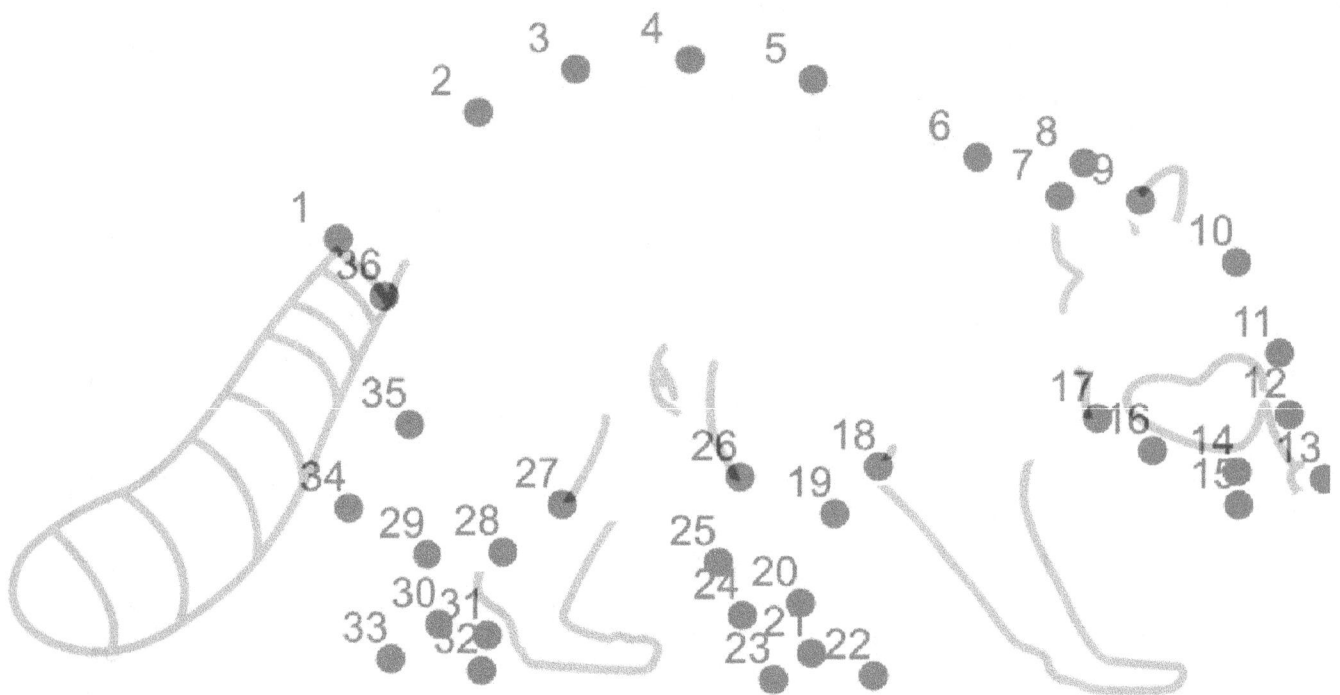

Are you an omnivore like a raccoon? An herbivore only eats plant foods. A carnivore only eats meat. An omnivore eats both. What type of eater are you? Write down some of your favorite foods to back up your answer.

_____

_____

24

# Black Canyon of the Gunnison
# Word Search

Words may be horizontal, vertical, diagonal,
or they might even be backwards!

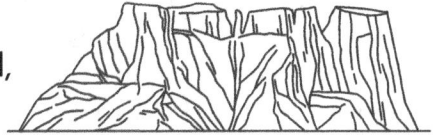

1. colorado
2. gunnison
3. rapids
4. gambel oak
5. owls
6. poison springhill
7. canyon wall
8. kolb
9. taylor
10. railroad
11. cimmarron
12. livestock
13. corrals
14. south rim
15. astronomy
16. fishing
17. scenic
18. kayaking
19. vertical
20. montrose
21. curecanti

```
C U R E C A N T I S G L O W K
P T O S R C O L O R A D O M J
O W L S A A O S C C M B C O A
I M Y C G P P K O L B L I N S
S E A E I S V I O E E U M T T
O O T N T L O A D C L C M R R
N E S I E A E K I S O A A O O
S L B C M R I E G W A N R S N
P E H S G R L O B E K Y R E O
R A I L R O A D H I P O O E M
I T A H C C I N O O K N N V Y
N L I V E S T O C K O W I E E
G N I H S I F R E S C A L R W
H C S O U T H R I M O L V T H
I I C A K M I N E R A L H I A
L T T F M E N T A H S E Q C L
L Y D R O U L E C T R I C A E
C J D O G K A Y A K I N G L M
```

25

# Wildlife Wisdom

The national park is home to many different kinds of animals. Seeing wildlife can be an exciting part of visiting the national park but it is important to remember that these animals are wild. They need plenty of space and a healthy habitat where they can find their own food. Part of this is not allowing animals to eat any human food. This is their home and we are the visitors. We need to be respectful of the wildlife in the park.

Directions: Circle the highlighted words that best complete the following sentences.

If an animal changes its behavior because of your presence, you are:
A) too close
B) funny looking
C) dehydrated and should drink more water

The best thing we can do to help wild animals survive is:
A) make them pets
B) protect their habitat
C) knit them winter sweaters

In a national park, it is okay to share your food with wild animals:
A) never
B) always
C) sometimes

When you're hiking in an area where there are bears, you should warn bears that you are entering their space by:
A) hiking quietly
B) making noise
C) wearing bright colors

At night, park rangers care for the animals by:
A) putting them back into their cages
B) tucking them into bed
C) leaving them alone

If you see an abandoned bird's nest, it is best to:
A) pet the baby birds
B) leave it alone
C) crunch the empty eggshells

Bears look under logs in hopes of finding:
A) granola bars
B) insects
C) peanuts to eat

The place where an animal lives is called its:
A) condo
B) habitat
C) crib

26

# Camping Packing List

What should you take with you when you go camping? Pretend you are in charge of your family camping trip. Make a list of what you would need to be safe and comfortable on an overnight excursion. Some considerations are listed on the side.

1.
2.
3.
4.
5.
6.
7.
8.
9.
10.
11.
12.
13.
14.
15.
16.

- What will you eat at every meal?

- What will the weather be like?

- Where will you sleep?

- What will you do during your free time?

- How luxurious do you want your camp to be?

- How will you cook?

- How will you see at night?

- How will you dispose of trash?

- What might you need in case of emergencies?

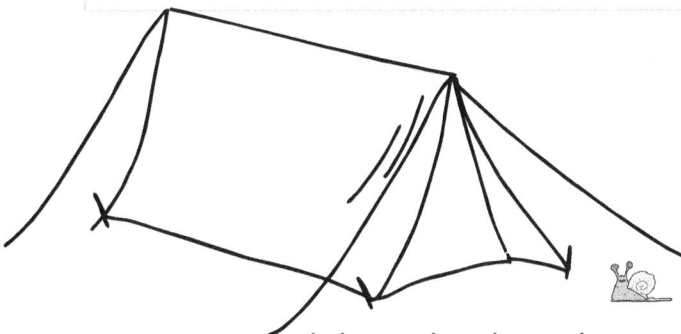

There are two campgrounds located in the park, one on the north rim and one on the south rim. If you are up for a more rugged adventure, camping in the canyon will require a permit.

# The Perfect Picnic Spot

Fill in the blanks on this page without looking at the full story. Once you have each line filled out, use the words you've chosen to complete the story on the next page.

EMOTION _____

FOOD _____

SOMETHING SWEET _____

STORE _____

MODE OF TRANSPORTATION _____

NOUN _____

SOMETHING ALIVE _____

SAUCE _____

PLURAL VEGETABLES _____

ADJECTIVE _____

PLURAL BODY PART _____

ANIMAL _____

PLURAL FRUIT _____

PLACE _____

SOMETHING TALL _____

COLOR _____

ADJECTIVE _____

NOUN _____

A DIFFERENT ANIMAL _____

FAMILY MEMBER #1 _____

FAMILY MEMBER #2 _____

VERB THAT ENDS IN -ING _____

A DIFFERENT FOOD _____

# The Perfect Picnic Spot

Use the words from the previous page to complete a silly story.

When my family suggested having our lunch at Gunnison Point, I was

_____. I love eating my _____ outside! I knew we had picked up a
EMOTION                FOOD

box of _____ from the _____ for after lunch, my favorite. We drove up
SOMETHING SWEET      STORE

to the area and I jumped out of the _____. "I will find the perfect spot for
MODE OF TRANSPORTATION

a picnic!" I grabbed a _____ for us to sit on, and I ran off. I passed a picnic
NOUN

table, but it was covered with _____ so we couldn't sit there. The next
SOMETHING ALIVE

picnic table looked okay, but there were smears of _____ and pieces of
SAUCE

_____ everywhere. The people that were there before must have been
PLURAL VEGETABLES

_____! I gritted my _____ together and kept walking down the path,
ADJECTIVE      PLURAL BODY PART

determined to find the perfect spot. I wanted a table with a good view of the

canyon. Why was this so hard? If we were lucky, I might even get to see _____
ANIMAL

eating some _____ on the cliffside. They don't have those in _____, where
PLURAL FRUIT               PLACE

I am from. I walked down a little hill and there it was, the perfect spot! The

trees towered overhead and looked as tall as _____. The patch of grass
SOMETHING TALL

was a beautiful _____ color. The _____ flowers were growing on
COLOR        ADJECTIVE

the side of a _____. I looked across the canyons edge and even saw a
NOUN

_____ on the edge of a rock. I looked back to see my _____ and
DIFFERENT ANIMAL            FAMILY MEMBER #1

_____ _____ a picnic basket. "I hope you brought plenty of
FAMILY MEMBER #2    VERB THAT ENDS IN ING

_____, I'm starving!"
A DIFFERENT FOOD

29

# Hike the Cedar Point Nature Trail

start here →

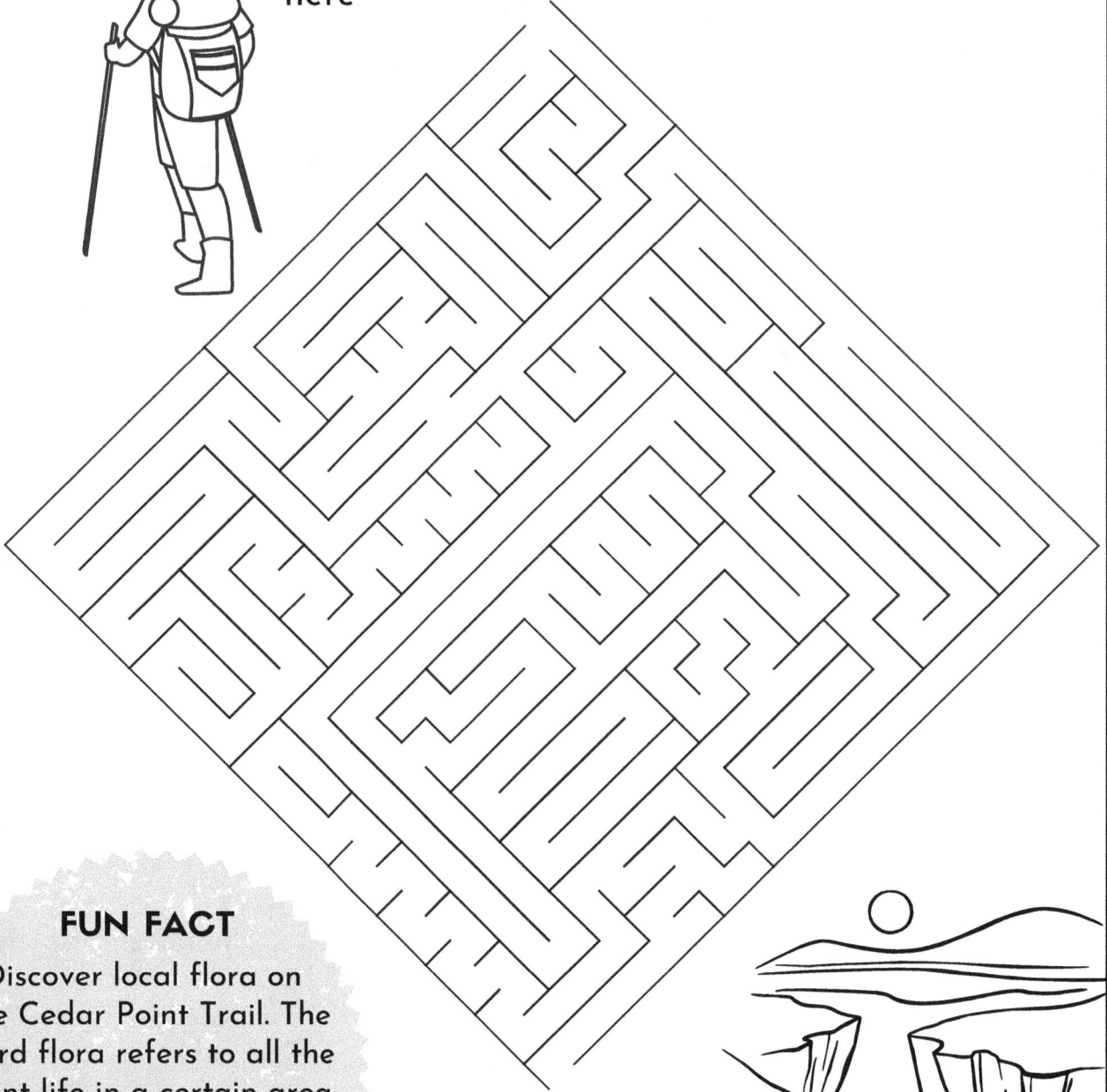

**FUN FACT**

Discover local flora on the Cedar Point Trail. The word flora refers to all the plant life in a certain area. This trail has guideposts describing the various plants along the way.

# Rock Scrambling
# Word Search

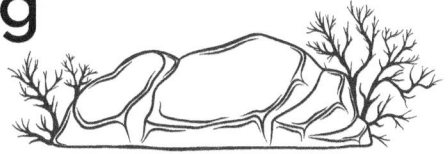

Rock scrambling is a method of climbing up boulders and rocks using both your hands and your feet. The inner canyon offers several areas where people can do this challenging sport!

1. balance
2. tricky
3. ascent
4. stones
5. dirty
6. gravity
7. steep
8. terrain
9. trail
10. technique
11. trekking
    poles
12. unmarked
13. poison ivy
14. pants
15. vertical
16. walls

```
L D E T E C H N I Q U E P W C
H A D A M I A Z P W A E W R H
D I R T Y I T T O W E L K O A
S E U D S P T U I T U T B S T
B A L A N C E A S E Y R C K R
M P D L P R K O T A E I O E
C O S E A R R E N H N R Y A K
S R B E N K A R I T L S T N K
E T H O T I I O V L U D I P I
N O I R S M N Y Y G U G V T N
O S A U A T I C N N K B A C G
T R I C K Y O I S D S K R R P
S J O S F H I N Z I I L G O O
E Y T R A I L E I N D R V S L
R W E L D O R A D O A O H L E
T T V E R T I C A L A K E L S
U A E E S A E N N O A P V A B
U N M A R K E D R C Y S I W N
```

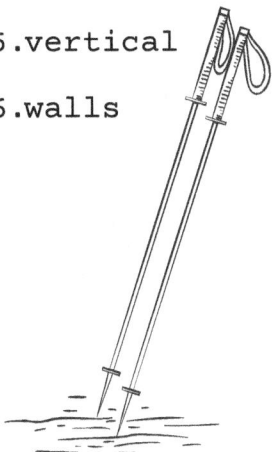

# Leave No Trace Quiz

Leave No Trace is a concept that helps people make decisions during outdoor recreation that protects the environment. There are seven principles that guide us when we spend time outdoors, whether you are in a national park or not. Are you an expert in Leave No Trace? Take this quiz and find out!

1. How can you plan ahead and prepare to ensure you have the best experience you can in the national park?
    a. Make sure you stop by the ranger station for a map and to ask about current conditions.
    b. Just wing it! You will know the best trail when you see it.
    c. Stick to your plan, even if conditions change. You traveled a long way to get here, and you should stick to your plan.
2. What is an example of traveling on a durable surface?
    a. Walking only on the designated path.
    b. Walking on the grass that borders the trail if the trail is very muddy.
    c. Taking a shortcut if you can find one because it means you will be walking less.
3. Why should you dispose of waste properly?
    a. You don't need to. Park rangers love to pick up the trash you leave behind.
    b. You should actually leave your leftovers behind, because animals will eat them. It is important to make sure they aren't hungry.
    c. So that other peoples' experiences of the park are not impacted by you leaving your waste behind.
4. How can you best follow the concept "leave what you find?"
    a. Take only a small rock or leaf to remember your trip.
    b. Take pictures, but leave any physical items where they are.
    c. Leave everything you find, unless it may be rare like an arrowhead, then it is okay to take.
5. What is not a good example of minimizing campfire impacts?
    a. Only having a campfire in a pre-existing campfire ring.
    b. Checking in with current conditions when you consider making a campfire.
    c. Building a new campfire ring in a location that has a better view.
6. What is a poor example of respecting wildlife?
    a. Building squirrel houses out of rocks so the squirrels have a place to live.
    b. Stay far away from wildlife and give them plenty of space.
    c. Reminding your grown-ups not to drive too fast in animal habitats while visiting the park.
7. How can you show consideration of other visitors?
    a. Play music on your speaker so other people at the campground can enjoy it.
    b. Wear headphones on the trail if you choose to listen to music.
    c. Make sure to yell "Hello!" to every animal you see at top volume.

# Park Poetry

America's parks inspire art of all kinds. Painters, sculptors, photographers, writers, and artists of all mediums have taken inspiration from natural beauty. They have turned their inspiration into great works.

Use this space to write your own poem about the park. Think about what you have experienced or seen. Use descriptive language to create an acrostic poem. This type of poem has the first letter of each line spell out another word. Create an acrostic that spells out the word "Canyon."

**C** _____

**A** _____

**N** _____

**Y** _____

**O** _____

**N** _____

**C** liffs

**A** s far as I can see

**N** ew adventures

**Y** ipee!

**O** asis

**N** othing like it

**C** oyotes howl

**A** ll around

**N** othing but stars

**Y** esterday an

**O** dyssey

**N** ow, night

# Bear Aware

Bears in the wild have plenty of things to eat! When you are in bear country, it is especially important to keep bears safe by making sure they can't eat any human food. When you are camping, you should store your food in special bear boxes. These metal storage boxes are animal-proof and will prevent wildlife from getting to your food.

Draw a line from each item to either the bear (if it is safe for bears to eat it) or to the bear box (if it needs to be stored.)

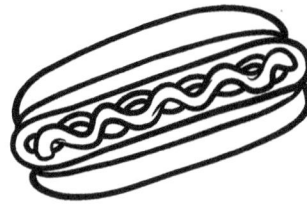

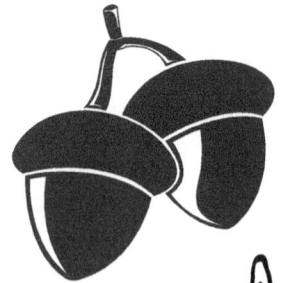

# Catch a Fish in the Gunnison River

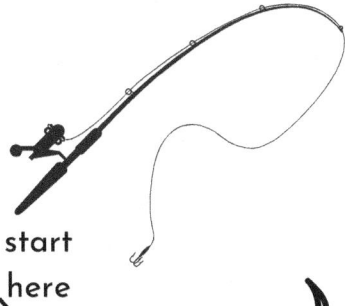

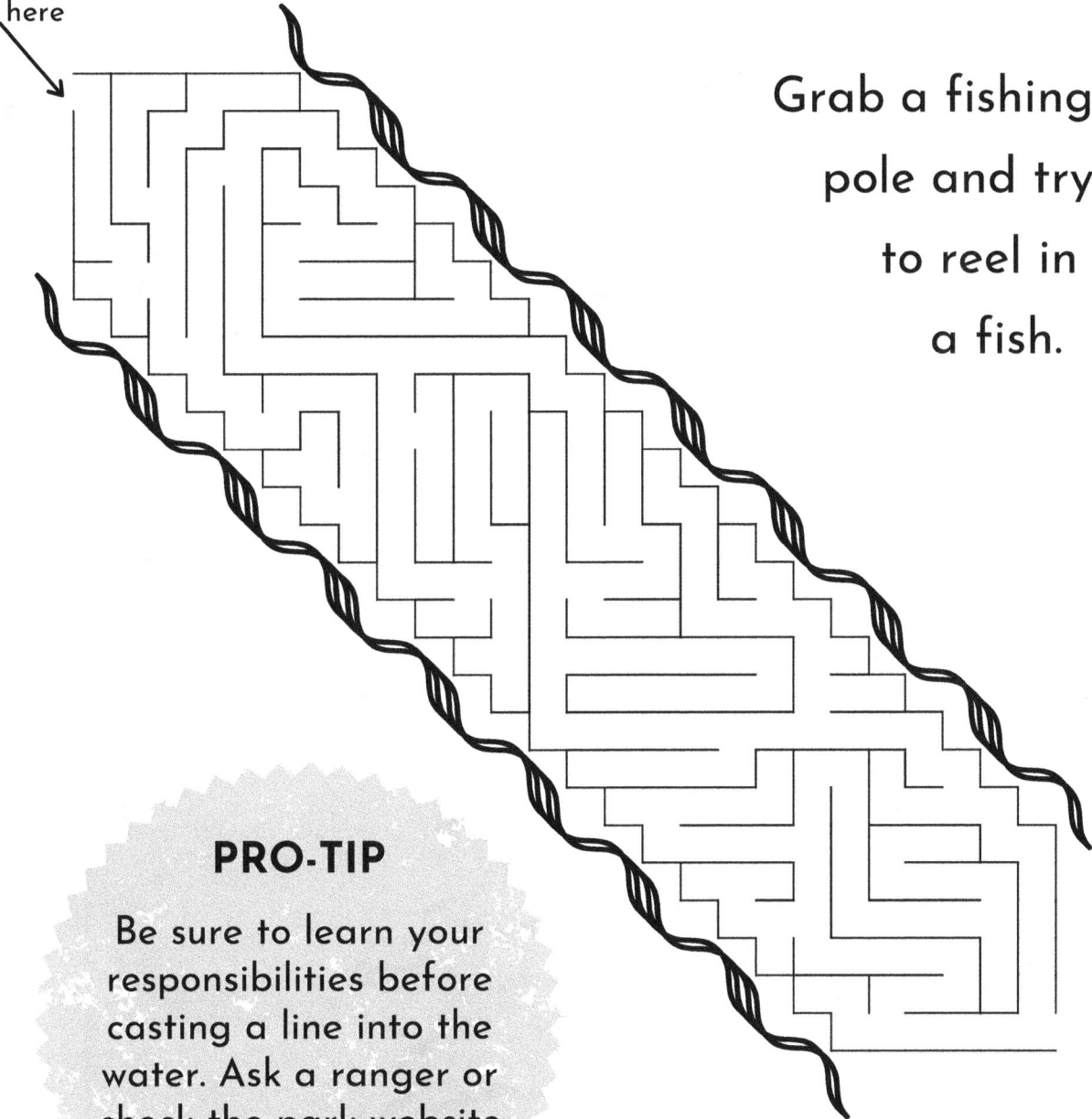

start
here

Grab a fishing
pole and try
to reel in
a fish.

## PRO-TIP

Be sure to learn your
responsibilities before
casting a line into the
water. Ask a ranger or
check the park website
before you go.

# Stacking Rocks

Have you ever seen stacks of rocks while hiking in national parks? Do you know what they are or what they mean? These rock piles are called cairns and often mark hiking routes in parks. Every park has a different way to maintain trails and cairns. However, they all have the same rule: If you come across a cairn, do not disturb it!

Color the cairn and the rules to remember.

## 1. Do not tamper with cairns.

If a cairn is tampered with or an unauthorized one is built, then future visitors may become disoriented or even lost.

## 2. Do not build unauthorized cairns.

Moving rocks disturbs the soil and makes the area more prone to erosion. Disturbing rocks can disturb fragile plants.

## 3. Do not add to existing cairns.

Authorized cairns are carefully designed. Adding to them can actually cause them to collapse.

# Decoding Using American Sign Language

American Sign Language, also called ASL for short, is a language that many Deaf people or people who are hard of hearing use to communicate. People use ASL to communicate with their hands. Did you know people from all over the country and world travel to national parks? You may hear people speaking other languages. You might also see people using ASL. Use the American Manual Alphabet chart to decode some national parks facts.

**This was the first national park to be established:**

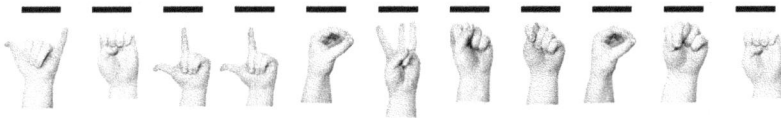

_ _ _ _ _ _ _ _ _ _

**This is the biggest national park in the US:**

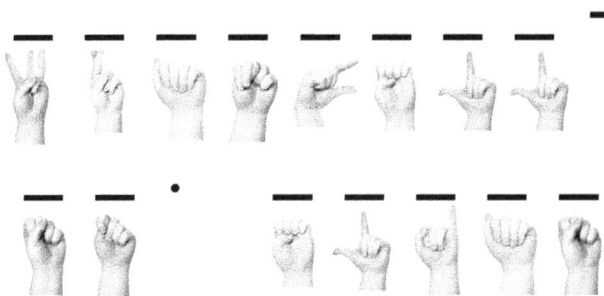

_ _ _ _ _ -

_ _ . _ _ _ _

**This is the most visited national park:**

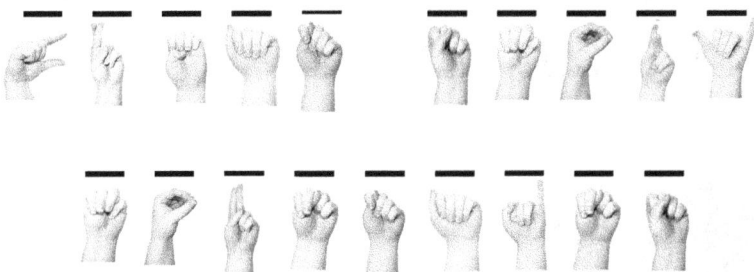

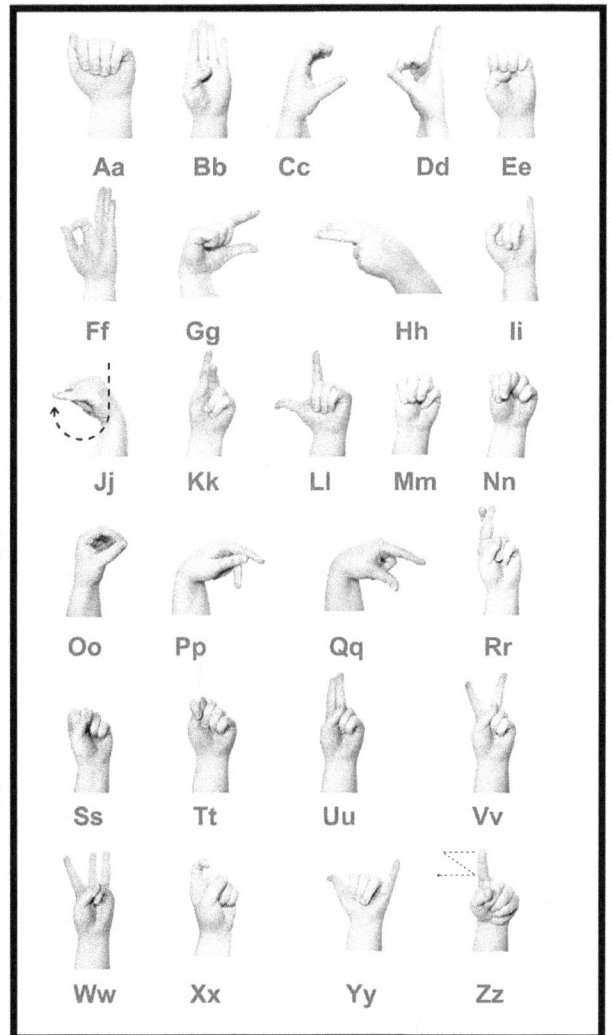

_ _ _ _ _ _ _ _ _

_ _ _ _ _ _

**American Manual Alphabet Chart**

Aa Bb Cc Dd Ee
Ff Gg Hh Ii
Jj Kk Ll Mm Nn
Oo Pp Qq Rr
Ss Tt Uu Vv
Ww Xx Yy Zz

Hint: Pay close attention to the position of the thumb!

Try it! Using the chart, try to make the letters of the alphabet with your hand. What is the hardest letter to make? Can you spell out your name? Show a friend or family member and have them watch you spell out the name of the national park you are in.

# Go Birdwatching at Exclamation Point

start
here

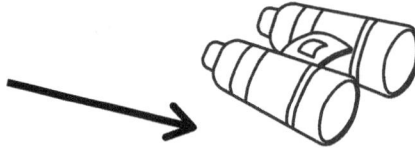

# Butterflies of Black Canyon

Dozens of species of butterflies and moths live in Black Canyon of the Gunnison National Park. Their wingspan size varies, as do the patterns on their wings. Design your own butterfly below. Make sure the wings are symmetrical, which means both sides match.

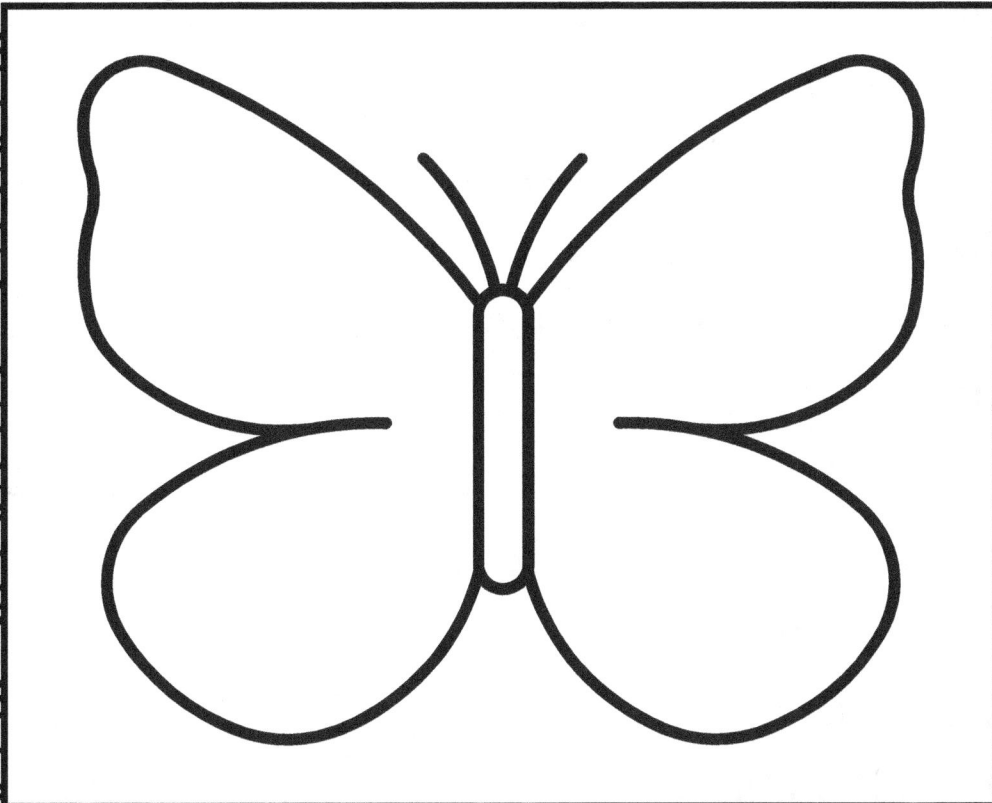

# A Hike at Rim Rock Trail

Fill in the blanks on this page without looking at the full story. Once you have each line filled out, use the words you've chosen to complete the story on the next page.

ADJECTIVE _____

SOMETHING TO EAT _____

SOMETHING TO DRINK _____

NOUN _____

ARTICLE OF CLOTHING _____

BODY PART _____

VERB _____

ANIMAL _____

SAME TYPE OF FOOD _____

ADJECTIVE _____

SAME ANIMAL _____

VERB THAT ENDS IN "ED" _____

NUMBER _____

A DIFFERENT NUMBER _____

SOMETHING THAT FLIES _____

LIGHT SOURCE _____

PLURAL NOUN _____

FAMILY MEMBER _____

YOUR NICKNAME _____

# A Hike at Rim Rock Trail

Use the words from the previous page to complete a silly story.

I went for a hike at Rim Rock trail. In my favorite _ _ _ _ _ _ _ backpack, I made
ADJECTIVE

sure to pack a map so I wouldn't get lost. I also threw in an extra

_ _ _ _ _ _ _ _ _ _ just in case I got hungry and a bottle of _ _ _ _ _ _ _ _ _ _ . I put
SOMETHING TO EAT                                                                    SOMETHING TO DRINK

on my _ _ _ _ _ _ _ _ _ spray, and I tied a _ _ _ _ _ _ _ _ _ _ _ around my
NOUN                                                      ARTICLE OF CLOTHING

_ _ _ _ _ _ _ _ _ , in case it gets chilly. I started to _ _ _ _ _ _ down the path. As
BODY PART                                                                    VERB

soon as I turned the corner, I came face to face with a(n) _ _ _ _ _ _ _ _ . I think
ANIMAL

it was as startled as I was! What should I do? I had to think fast! Should I

give it some of my _ _ _ _ _ _ _ _ _ _ ? No. I had to remember what the
SAME TYPE OF FOOD

_ _ _ _ _ _ _ ranger told me: "If you see one, back away slowly and try not to
ADJECTIVE

scare it." Soon enough, the _ _ _ _ _ _ _ _ _ _     _ _ _ _ _ _ _ _ _ _ away. The coast
SAME ANIMAL          VERB THAT ENDS IN ED

was clear. _ _ _ _ _ _ hours later, I finally reached the lookout. I felt like I could
NUMBER

see for a _ _ _ _ _ _ miles. I took a picture of a _ _ _ _ _ _ _ _ so I could always
A DIFFERENT NUMBER                    NOUN

remember this moment. As I was putting my camera away, a _ _ _ _ _ _ _ _ _
SOMETHING THAT FLIES

flew by, reminding me that it was almost nighttime. I turned on my

_ _ _ _ _ _ _ _ _ _ and headed back. I could hear the _ _ _ _ _ _ _ _ _ _ singing their
LIGHT SOURCE                                          PLURAL INSECT

evening song. Just as I was getting tired, I saw my _ _ _ _ _ _ _ _ _ _ and our tent.
FAMILY MEMBER

"Welcome back _ _ _ _ _ _ _ _ ! How was your hike?"
NICKNAME

# Rain, Rain, Rain

If it rains while you are visiting Black Canyon of the Gunnison National Park, you can do this activity during your trip. If you don't get any rain while you are there, you can follow the same instructions next time it rains where you live.

Go outside into the rain. Use all of your senses as you complete the boxes below. You can use words, drawings, or both.

Sit as still as you can and listen to the rain. How does it make you feel?

Look straight up at the sky and let the raindrops fall on your face. Close your eyes. How does it feel?

Watch where the rain goes. Pay attention to the different surfaces the rain lands on. Which surfaces absorb the rain, and which surfaces cause the rain to run off or pool?

Are there any animals or bugs out enjoying the rain? Do you think the plants are enjoying the rain?

# Let's Go Camping Word Search

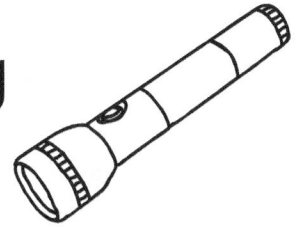

Words may be horizontal, vertical, diagonal, or they might even be backwards!

1. tent
2. camp stove
3. sleeping bag
4. bug spray
5. sunscreen
6. map
7. flashlight
8. pillow
9. lantern
10. ice
11. snacks
12. smores
13. water
14. first aid kit
15. chair
16. cards
17. books
18. games
19. trail
20. hat

```
D P P I L L O W D B T E A C I
E O A D P R E A A M B R C A N
P W C A M P S T O V E I H X G
R A H S G E L E B E E D A P S
E L B U G S P R A Y N G I E A
S I A H G C I C N N M E R C N
C W N L A F I R S K O O B F K
M T A E M I L E L H M R W L J
T A P R E A O R E S L B A A B
S M P A S R R T E N T L U S C
C E A I I R C G P E I U J H A
S S N A C K S S I M O K I L R
I J R S F O I S N J R A Q I D
C Y E T L E V E G U O R V G S
E W T A K C A B B S S O H H M
X J N F I R S T A I D K I T T
U A A E S S E N G E T P V A B
C J L I A R T D N A M A H A S
```

43

# All in the Day of a Park Ranger

Park Rangers are hardworking individuals dedicated to protecting our parks, monuments, museums, and more. They take care of the natural and cultural resources for future generations. Rangers also help protect the visitors of the park. Their responsibilities are broad and they work both with the public and behind the scenes.

What have you seen park rangers do? Use your knowledge of the duties of park rangers to fill out a typical daily schedule, listing one activity for each hour. Feel free to make up your own, but some examples of activities are provided on the right. Read carefully! Not all the example activities are befitting a ranger.

| Time | Activity |
|------|----------|
| 6 am | Lead a sunrise hike |
| 7 am | |
| 8 am | |
| 9 am | |
| 10 am | |
| 11 am | |
| 12 pm | Enjoy a lunch break outside |
| 1 pm | |
| 2 pm | |
| 3 pm | |
| 4 pm | Teach visitors about the geology of the canyon |
| 5 pm | |
| 6 pm | |
| 7 pm | |
| 8 pm | |
| 9 pm | |

- feed the migratory birds
- build trails for visitors to enjoy
- throw rocks off the side of the canyon
- rescue lost hikers
- study animal behavior
- record air quality data
- answer questions at the visitor center
- pick wildflowers
- pick up litter
- share marshmallows with squirrels
- repair handrails
- lead a class on a field trip
- catch salamanders and make them race
- lead people on educational hikes
- write articles for the park website
- protect the river from pollution
- remove non-native plants from the park
- study how climate change is affecting the park
- give a talk about mountain lions
- lead a program for campers on rainbow trout

If you were a park ranger, which of the above tasks would you enjoy most?

_____

_____

# Draw Yourself as a Park Ranger

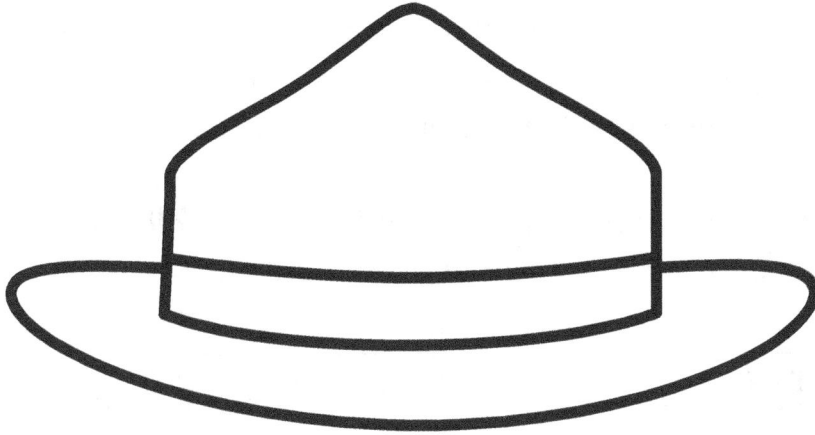

RANGER

# National Park Names

You may be familiar with places designated as a "national park" but this is just one way parks can be named. There are over 400 units (places) in the National Parks Service (NPS) and quite a few ways these places are titled. Certain qualities of parks are reflected in the variety of titles given to them, and these titles offer clues as to what you might find there. Besides the 63 national parks, there are national monuments, national scenic trails, national battlefields, and many more.

The letters of several designations of NPS units are all jumbled up. Can you unscramble the word and figure out the title?

**ERRIV**
○ ☐ ☐ R

**CETERYME**
○ M ☐ ☐ ☐ ☐

**SHSEAREO**
S ○ ○ ☐ ☐ ☐ E

**ESERVER**
○ S ☐ ☐ ☐ ☐

**ARWAYPK**
P ☐ ☐ ☐ ○ ☐

**MRIAEMOL**
☐ ○ ☐ ☐ ☐ A ☐

**RELASHOKE**
☐ A ☐ ☐ ○ R ☐

Now arrange the circled letters to solve one last type of NPS unit.

○ ○ ○ R ○ ○ T I ○ N ☐ A R ○ ○

46

# Star Messages

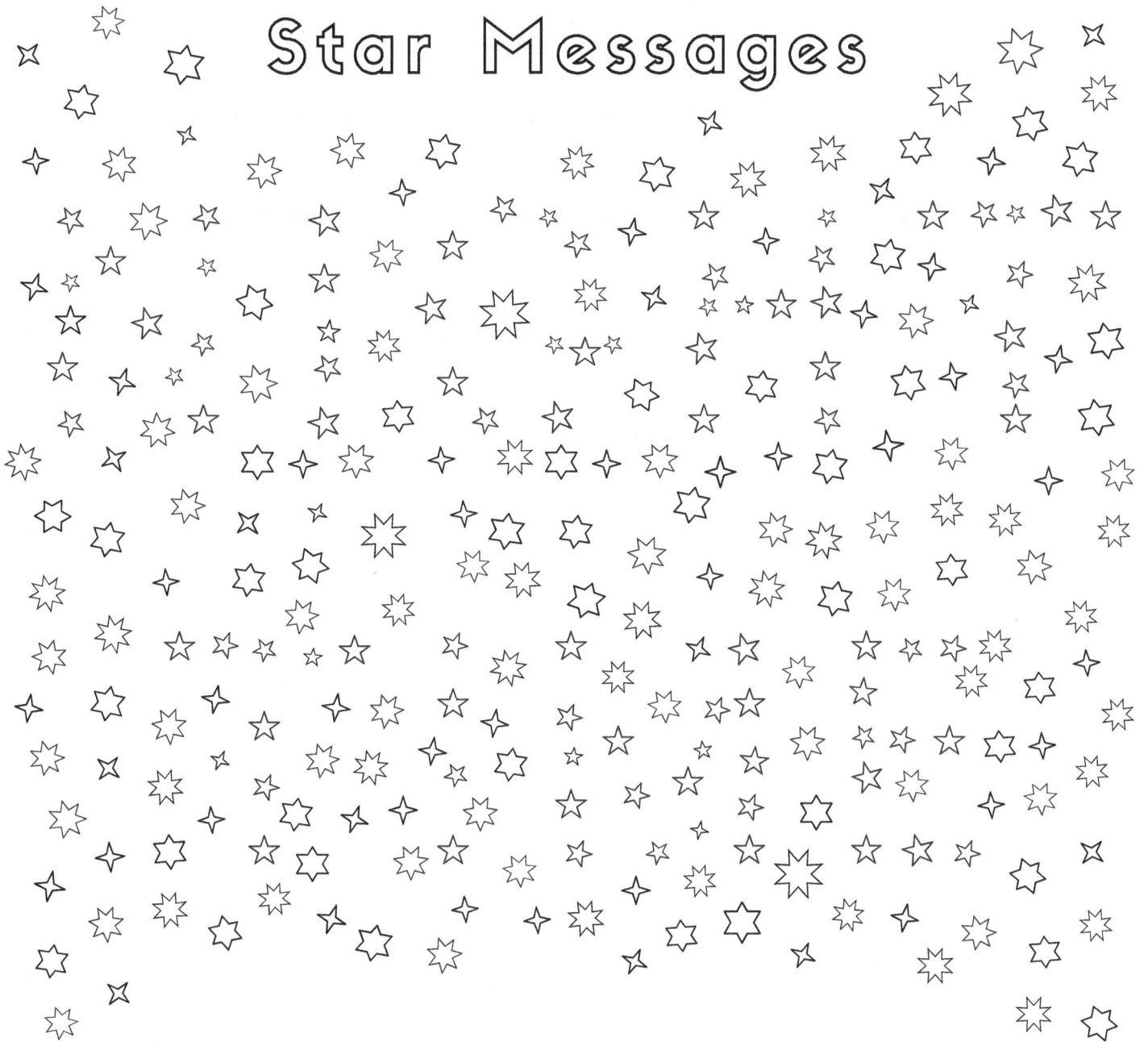

The ringtail or ringtail cat is a member of the raccoon family. They make their home in the Black Canyon and den in caves, rocky crevices, or hollow trees.

Color in all the stars with exactly 5 points to find out when these mammals are most active.

# Sound Exploration

Spend a minute or two listening to all of the sounds around you.
Draw your favorite sound.

How did this sound make you feel?

_____

_____

What did you think when you heard this sound?

_____

_____

# Take in the Teeny-Tiny

Take a walk through the park and draw examples of teensy things you can find like little plants, bugs, and pebbles.

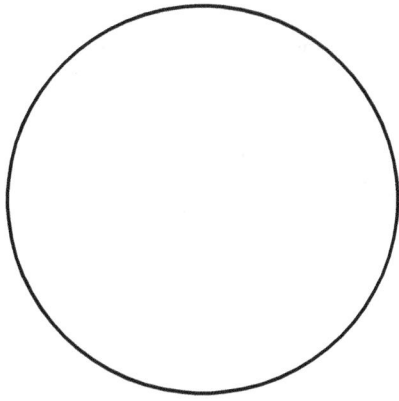

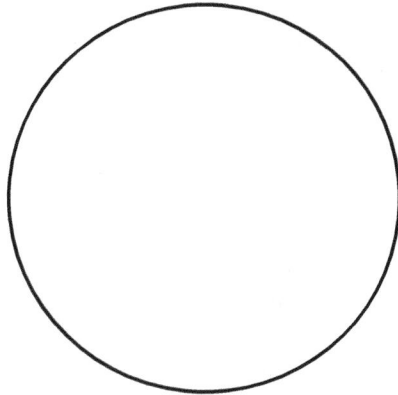

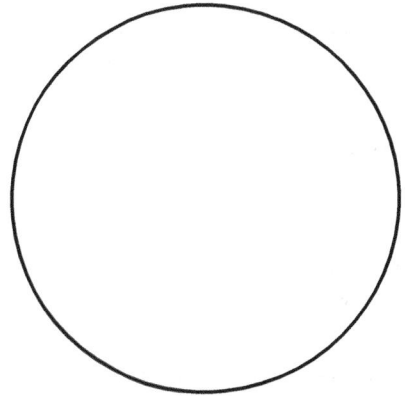

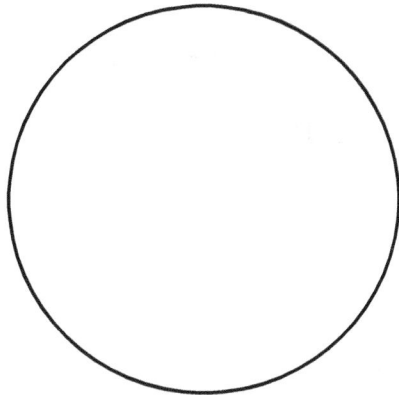

# 63 National Parks

How many other national parks have you been to? Which one do you want to visit next? Note that if some of these parks fall on the border of more than one state, you may check it off more than once!

## Alaska
- ☐ Denali National Park
- ☐ Gates of the Arctic National Park
- ☐ Glacier Bay National Park
- ☐ Katmai National Park
- ☐ Kenai Fjords National Park
- ☐ Kobuk Valley National Park
- ☐ Lake Clark National Park
- ☐ Wrangell-St. Elias National Park

## American Samoa
- ☐ National Park of American Samoa

## Arizona
- ☐ Grand Canyon National Park
- ☐ Petrified Forest National Park
- ☐ Saguaro National Park

## Arkansas
- ☐ Hot Springs National Park

## California
- ☐ Channel Islands National Park
- ☐ Death Valley National Park
- ☐ Joshua Tree National Park
- ☐ Kings Canyon National Park
- ☐ Lassen Volcanic National Park
- ☐ Pinnacles National Park
- ☐ Redwood National Park
- ☐ Sequoia National Park
- ☐ Yosemite National Park

## Colorado
- ☐ Black Canyon of the Gunnison National Park
- ☐ Great Sand Dunes National Park
- ☐ Mesa Verde National Park
- ☐ Rocky Mountain National Park

## Florida
- ☐ Biscayne National Park
- ☐ Dry Tortugas National Park
- ☐ Everglades National Park

## Hawaii
- ☐ Haleakalā National Park
- ☐ Hawai'i Volcanoes National Park

## Idaho
- ☐ Yellowstone National Park

## Kentucky
- ☐ Mammoth Cave National Park

## Indiana
- ☐ Indiana Dunes National Park

## Maine
- ☐ Acadia National Park

## Michigan
- ☐ Isle Royale National Park

## Minnesota
- ☐ Voyageurs National Park

## Missouri
- ☐ Gateway Arch National Park

## Montana
- ☐ Glacier National Park
- ☐ Yellowstone National Park

## Nevada
- ☐ Death Valley National Park
- ☐ Great Basin National Park

## New Mexico
- ☐ Carlsbad Caverns National Park
- ☐ White Sands National Park

## North Dakota
- ☐ Theodore Roosevelt National Park

## North Carolina
- ☐ Great Smoky Mountains National Park

## Ohio
- ☐ Cuyahoga Valley National Park

## Oregon
- ☐ Crater Lake National Park

## South Carolina
- ☐ Congaree National Park

## South Dakota
- ☐ Badlands National Park
- ☐ Wind Cave National Park

## Tennessee
- ☐ Great Smoky Mountains National Park

## Texas
- ☐ Big Bend National Park
- ☐ Guadalupe Mountains National Park

## Utah
- ☐ Arches National Park
- ☐ Bryce Canyon National Park
- ☐ Canyonlands National Park
- ☐ Capitol Reef National Park
- ☐ Zion National Park

## Virgin Islands
- ☐ Virgin Islands National Park

## Virginia
- ☐ Shenandoah National Park

## Washington
- ☐ Mount Rainier National Park
- ☐ North Cascades National Park
- ☐ Olympic National Park

## West Virginia
- ☐ New River Gorge National Park

## Wyoming
- ☐ Grand Teton National Park
- ☐ Yellowstone National Park

# Other National Parks Crossword

Besides Black Canyon of the Gunnison National Park, there are 62 other diverse and beautiful national parks across the United States. Try your hand at this crossword. If you need help, look at the previous page for some hints.

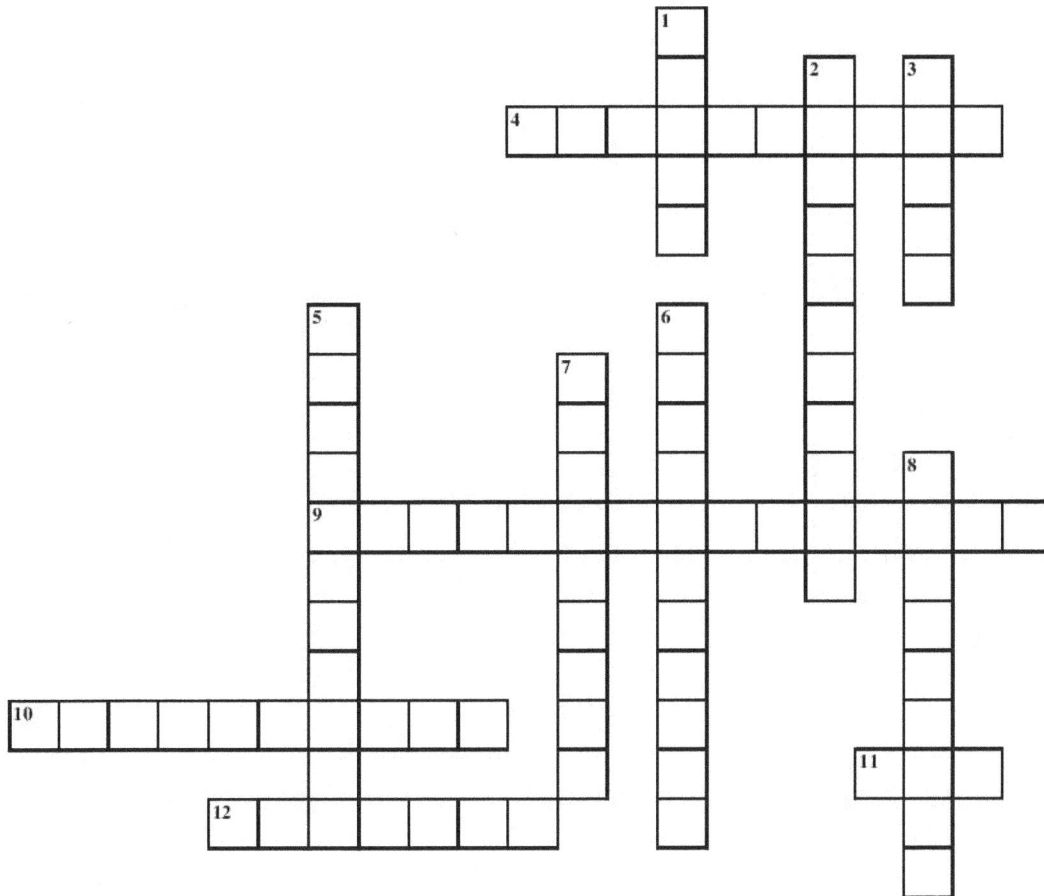

## Down

1. State where Acadia National Park is located
2. This national park has the Spanish word for turtle in it
3. Number of national parks in Alaska
5. This national park has some of the hottest temperatures in the world
6. This national park is the only one in Idaho
7. This toothsome creature can famously be found in Everglades National Park
8. Only president with a national park named for them

## Across

4. This state has the most national parks.
9. This park has some of the newest land in the US, caused by volcanic eruptions.
10. This park has the deepest lake in the United States.
11. This color shows up in the name of a national park in California.
12. This national park deserves a gold medal.

# Which National Park Will You Go To Next?
## Word Search

1. Zion
2. Big Bend
3. Glacier
4. Olympic
5. Sequoia
6. Bryce
7. Mesa Verde
8. Biscayne
9. Wind Cave
10. Great Basin
11. Katmai
12. Yellowstone
13. Voyageurs
14. Arches
15. Badlands
16. Denali
17. Glacier Bay
18. Hot Springs

```
F M M E S A V E R D E B N E Y
E A B I G B E N D E S A S E M
Y L I C A L O Y N E E D L T G
D M G A S S A U C N R L U E R
C E L I I T S C R E O A A K E
S N A W Y E E O I W T N A C A
G I C H A A Q C S E M D N S T
N O I Z P R U T I M R S N E B
I W E L M P O N B W E B K H A
R J R F D N I F L I H B U C S
P A B E E S A N E S O P W R I
S J A E N Y A C S I B A U A N
T C Y I A D O H H Y M E A L R
O T A T L M L E S E G R W R J
H S T O I K A T M A I R O P B
I C H U R C O L Y M P I C O U
O Y G T S D E O S B R Y C E T
W I N D C A V E I N R O H E M
```

52

# Field Notes

Spend some time reflecting on your trip to Black Canyon of the Gunnison National Park. Your field notes will help you remember the things you experienced. Use the space below to write about your day.

While I was at Black Canyon of the Gunnison National Park...

I saw:
_____
_____
_____
_____

I heard:
_____
_____
_____

I felt:
_____
_____

Draw a picture of your favorite thing in the park.

I wondered:

# ANSWER KEY

# Go Horseback Riding on the Deadhorse Trail

Help find the horse's lost shoe!

**DID YOU KNOW?**

Horseback riding is a popular activity in Black Canyon of the Gunnison National Park. There are many trails you can take horses for day or overnight trips.

start here →

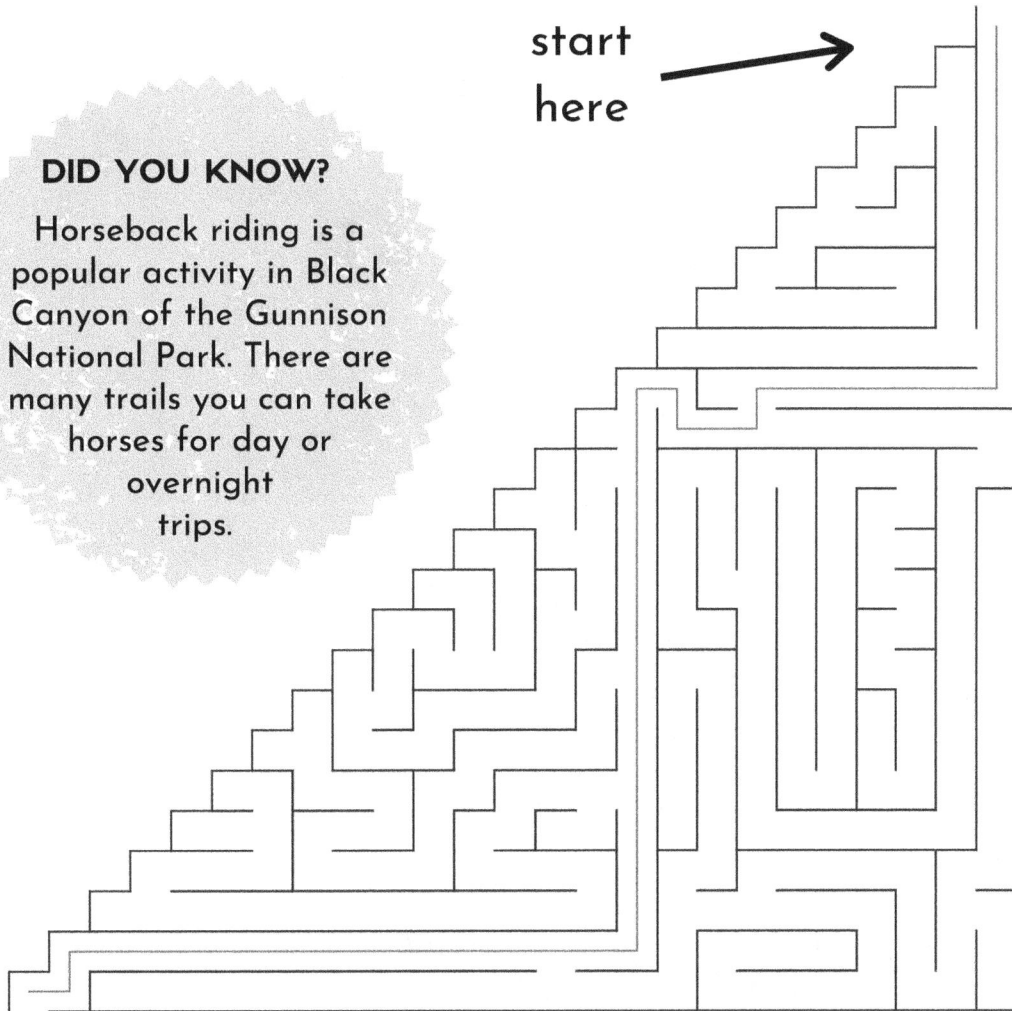

# Answers: Who lives here?

Below are 8 plants and animals that live in the park.
Use the word bank to fill in the clues below.

WORD BANK:   MILKSNAKE, DOUGLAS FIR, UTAH JUNIPER, MERLIN,
RINGTAIL, CHUKAR, MINK, OSPREY

RIN**G**TAIL

CH**U**KAR

MERLI**N**

UTAH ■JU**N**IPER

M**I**NK

DOUGLA**S** ■FIR

**O**SPREY

MILKS**N**AKE

# Common Names and Latin Names

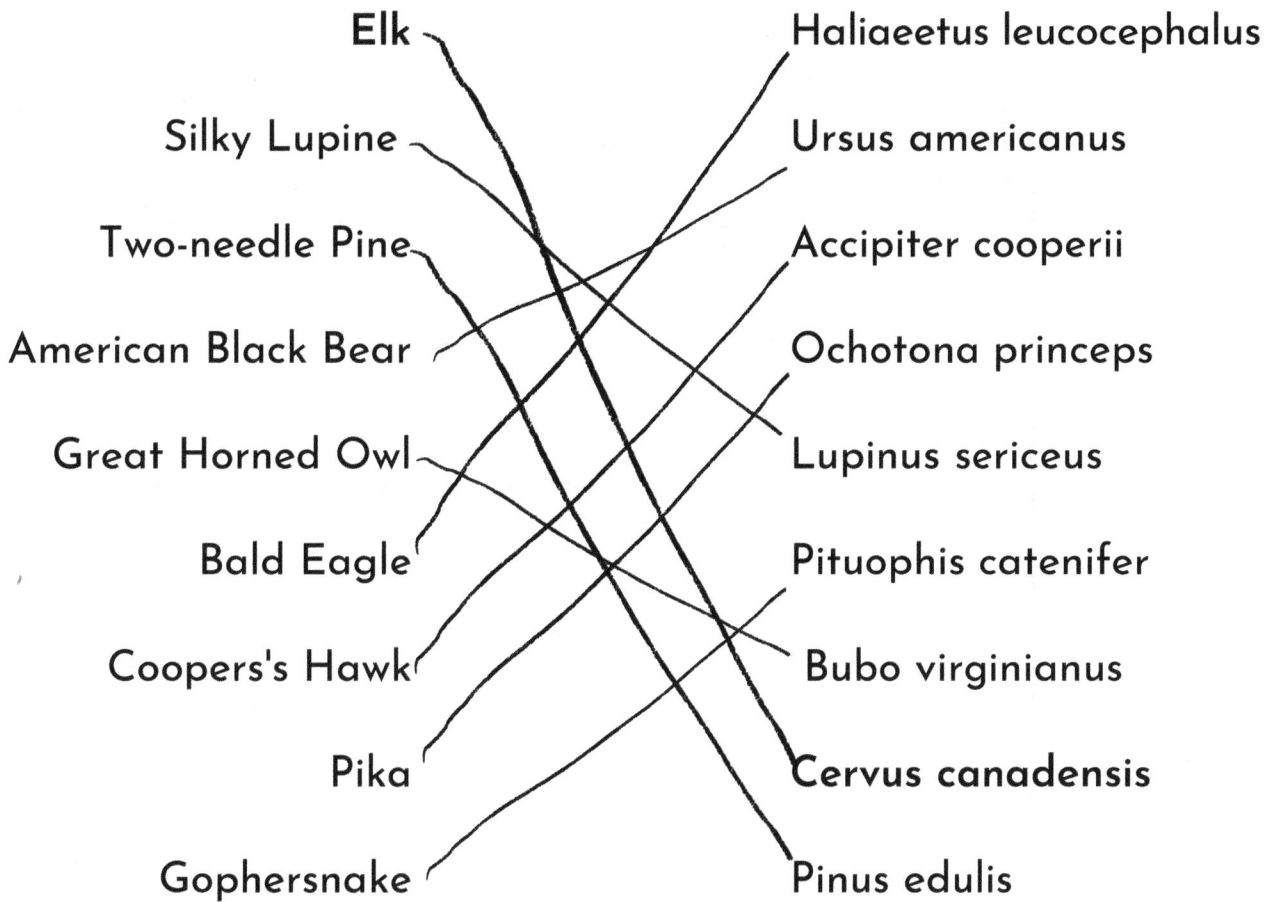

Elk — Haliaeetus leucocephalus

Silky Lupine — Ursus americanus

Two-needle Pine — Accipiter cooperii

American Black Bear — Ochotona princeps

Great Horned Owl — Lupinus sericeus

Bald Eagle — Pituophis catenifer

Coopers's Hawk — Bubo virginianus

Pika — Cervus canadensis

Gophersnake — Pinus edulis

# Jumbles Answers

1. FISHING

2. HIKING

3. BIRDING

4. CAMPING

5. PICNICKING

6. SIGHTSEEING

7. STAR GAZING

# Plotting Latitude and Longitude

| | 40°W | 30°W | 20°W | 10°W | 0° Prime Meridian | 10°E | 20°E | 30°E | 40°E |
|---|---|---|---|---|---|---|---|---|---|

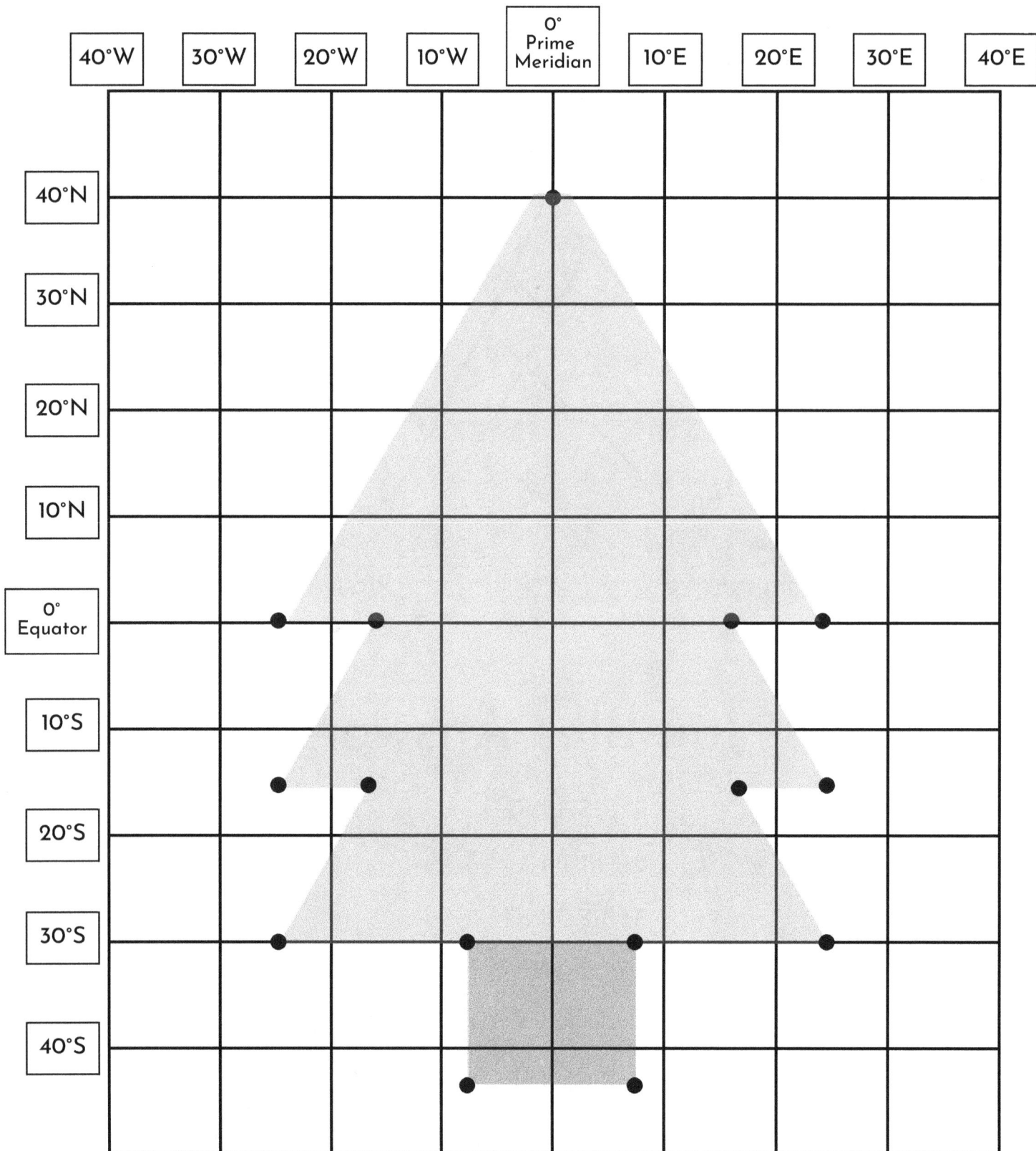

# National Park Emblem Answers

1. This represents all plants: **Sequoia Tree**

2. This represents all animals: **Bison**

3. This represents the landscapes: **Mountains**

4. This represents the waters protected by the park service: **Water**

5. This represents the historical and archeological values: **Arrowhead**

# Answers: The Ten Essentials

| | | | | |
|---|---|---|---|---|
| (fire: matches, lighter, tinder, and/or stove) | ~~a pint of milk~~ | ~~extra money~~ | (headlamp, plus extra batteries) | (extra clothes) |
| (extra water) | ~~a dog~~ | ~~Polaroid camera~~ | ~~bug net~~ | ~~lightweight game like a deck of cards~~ |
| (extra food) | ~~a roll of duct tape~~ | (shelter) | (sun protection, such as sunglasses, sun-protective clothes and sunscreen) | (knife, plus a gear repair kit) |
| ~~a mirror~~ | (navigation: map, compass, altimeter, GPS device, or satellite messenger) | (first aid kit) | ~~extra flip-flops~~ | ~~entertainment like video games or books~~ |

# Black Canyon of the Gunnison
# Word Search

Words may be horizontal, vertical, diagonal,
or they might even be backwards!

1. colorado
2. gunnison
3. rapids
4. gambel oak
5. owls
6. poison springhill
7. canyon wall
8. kolb
9. taylor
10. railroad
11. cimmarron
12. livestock
13. corrals
14. south rim
15. astronomy
16. fishing
17. scenic
18. kayaking
19. vertical
20. montrose
21. curecanti

```
C U R E C A N T I S G L O W K
P T O S R C O L O R A D O M J
O W L S A A O S C C M B C O A
I M Y C G P P K O L B L I N S
S E A E I S V I O E E U M T T
O O T N T L O A D C L C M R R
N E S I E A E K I S O A A O O
S L B C M R I E G W A N R S N
P E H S G R L O B E K Y R E O
R A I L R O A D H I P O O E M
I T A H C C I N O O K N N V Y
N L I V E S T O C K O W I E E
G N I H S I F R E S C A L R W
H C S O U T H R I M O L V T H
I I C A K M I N E R A L H I A
L T T F M E N T A O S E Q C L
L Y D R O U L E C T R I C A E
C J D O G K A Y A K I N G L M
```

60

# Wildlife Wisdom

The national park is home to many different kinds of animals. Seeing wildlife can be an exciting part of visiting the national park but it is important to remember that these animals are wild. They need plenty of space and a healthy habitat where they can find their own food. Part of this is not allowing animals to eat any human food. This is their home and we are the visitors. We need to be respectful of the wildlife in the park.

**Directions: Circle the highlighted words that best complete the following sentences.**

If an animal changes its behavior because of your presence, you are:
   A) too close
   B) funny looking
   C) dehydrated and should drink more water

The best thing we can do to help wild animals survive is:
   A) make them pets
   B) protect their habitat
   C) knit them winter sweaters

In a national park, it is okay to share your food with wild animals:
   A) never
   B) always
   C) sometimes

When you're hiking in an area where there are bears, you should warn bears that you are entering their space by:
   A) hiking quietly
   B) making noise
   C) wearing bright colors

At night, park rangers care for the animals by:
   A) putting them back into their cages
   B) tucking them into bed
   C) leaving them alone

If you see an abandoned bird's nest, it is best to:
   A) pet the baby birds
   B) leave it alone
   C) crunch the empty eggshells

Bears look under logs in hopes of finding:
   A) granola bars
   B) insects
   C) peanuts to eat

The place where an animal lives is called its:
   A) condo
   B) habitat
   C) crib

61

# Solution: Hike the Cedar Point Nature Trail

## FUN FACT

Discover local flora on the Cedar Point Trail. The word flora refers to all the plant life in a certain area. This trail has guideposts describing the various plants along the way.

# Rock Scrambling Word Search

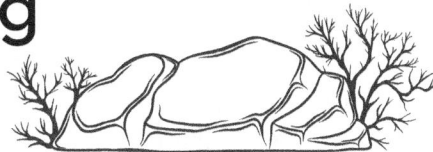

Rock scrambling is a method of climbing up boulders and rocks using both your hands and your feet. The inner canyon offers several areas where people can do this challenging sport!

1. balance
2. tricky
3. ascent
4. stones
5. dirty
6. gravity
7. steep
8. terrain
9. trail
10. technique
11. trekking poles
12. unmarked
13. poison ivy
14. pants
15. vertical
16. walls

```
L D E T E C H N I Q U E P W C
H A D A M I A Z P W A E W R H
D I R T Y I T T O W E L K O A
S E U D S P T U I T U T B S T
B A L A N C E A S E Y R C K R
M P D L P R K O T A E I O E
C O S E A R R E N H N R Y A K
S R B E N K A R I T L S T N K
E T H O T I I O V L U D I P I
N O I R S M N Y Y J U G V T N
O S A U A T I C N N K B A C G
T R I C K Y O I S D S K R R P
S J O S F H I N Z I I L G O O
E Y T R A I L E I N D R V S L
R W E L D O R A D O A O H L E
T T V E R T I C A L A K E L S
U A E E S A E N N O A P V A B
U N M A R K E D R C Y S I W N
```

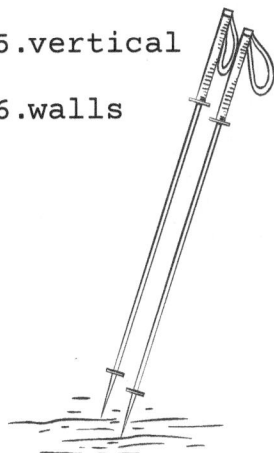

63

# Answers: Leave No Trace Quiz

1. How can you plan ahead and prepare to ensure you have the best experience you can in the National Park?

    A. Make sure you stop by the ranger station for a map and to ask about current conditions.

2. What is an example of traveling on a durable surface?

    A. Walking only on the designated path.

3. Why should you dispose of waste properly?

    C. So that other peoples' experiences of the park are not impacted by you leaving your waste behind.

4. How can you best follow the concept "leave what you find?"

    B. Take pictures but leave any physical items where they are.

5. What is not a good example of minimizing campfire impacts?

    C. Building a new campfire ring in a location that has a better view.

6. What is a poor example of respecting wildlife?

    A. Building squirrel houses out of rocks from the river so the squirrels have a place to live.

7. How can you show consideration of other visitors?

    B. Wear headphones on the trail if you choose to listen to music.

# Bear Aware

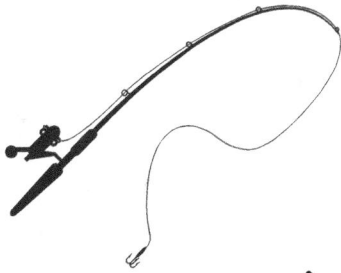

# Solution: Catch a Fish in the Gunnison River

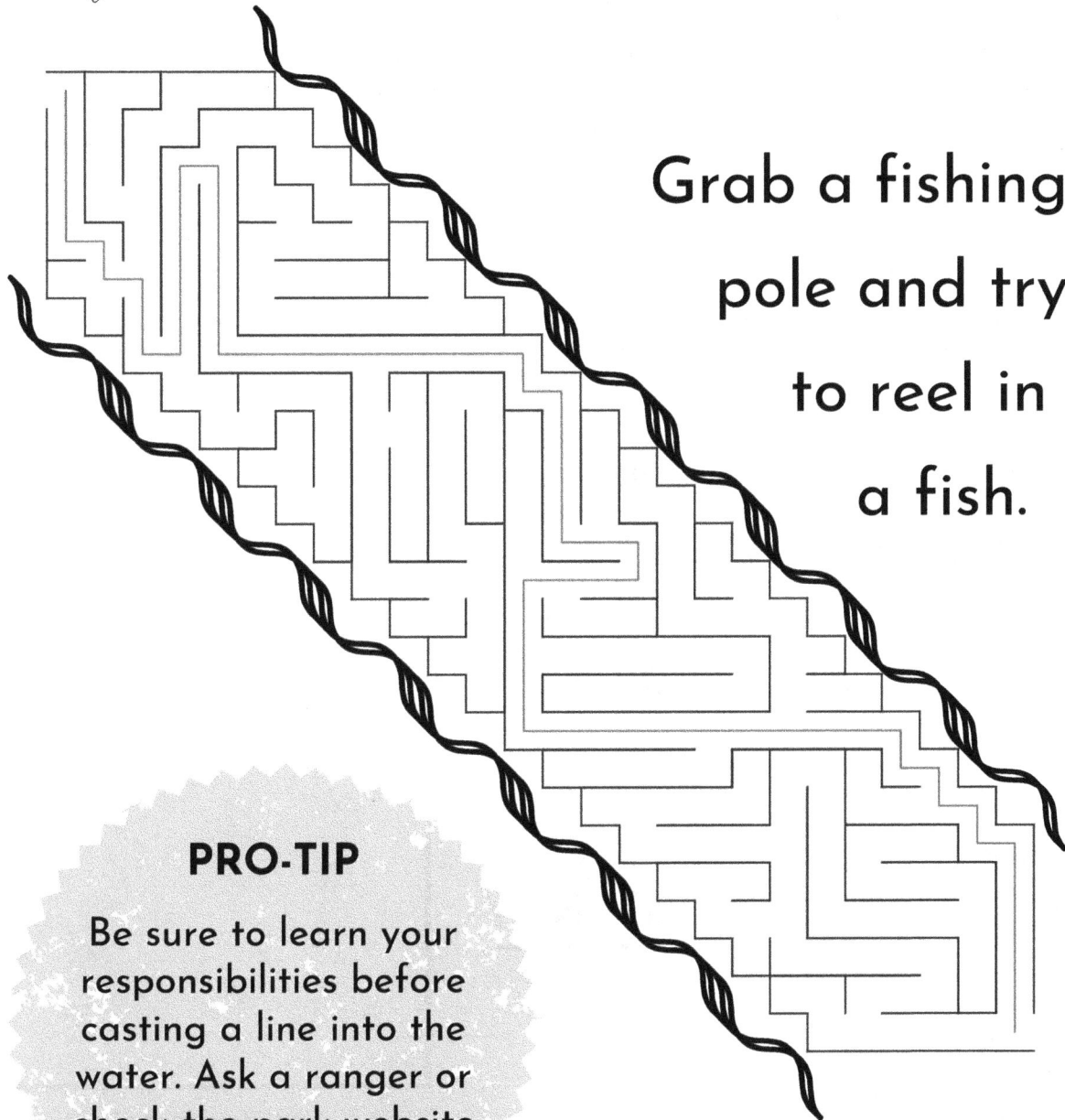

Grab a fishing pole and try to reel in a fish.

## PRO-TIP

Be sure to learn your responsibilities before casting a line into the water. Ask a ranger or check the park website before you go.

# Decoding Using American Sign Language

American Sign Language, also called ASL for short, is a language that many Deaf people or people who are hard of hearing use to communicate. People use ASL to communicate with their hands. Did you know people from all over the country and world travel to national parks? You may hear people speaking other languages. You might also see people using ASL. Use the American Manual Alphabet chart to decode some national parks facts.

This was the first national park to be established:

**Y E L L O W S T O N E**

This is the biggest national park in the US:

**W R A N G E L L -**

**S T . E L I A S**

This is the most visited national park:

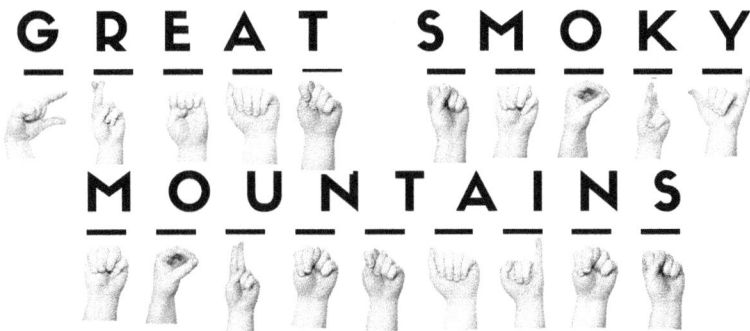

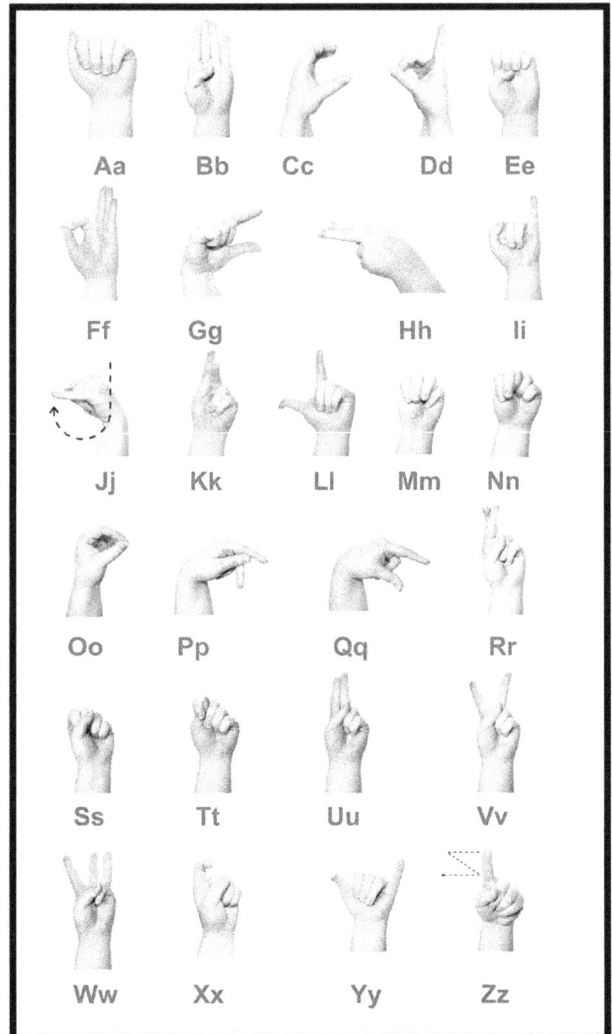

**G R E A T   S M O K Y**

**M O U N T A I N S**

| | | | | |
|---|---|---|---|---|
| Aa | Bb | Cc | Dd | Ee |
| Ff | Gg | | Hh | Ii |
| Jj | Kk | Ll | Mm | Nn |
| Oo | Pp | | Qq | Rr |
| Ss | Tt | Uu | | Vv |
| Ww | Xx | | Yy | Zz |

Hint: Pay close attention to the position of the thumb!

Try it! Using the chart, try to make the letters of the alphabet with your hand. What is the hardest letter to make? Can you spell out your name? Show a friend or family member and have them watch you spell out the name of the national park you are in.

# Go Birdwatching at Exclamation Point

start here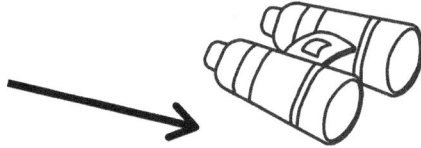

# Let's Go Camping
# Word Search

1. tent
2. camp stove
3. sleeping bag
4. bug spray
5. sunscreen
6. map
7. flashlight
8. pillow
9. lantern
10. ice
11. snacks
12. smores
13. water
14. first aid kit
15. chair
16. cards
17. books
18. games
19. trail
20. hat

```
D P P I L L O W D B T E A C I
E O A D P R E A A M B R C A N
P W C A M P S T O V E I H X G
R A H S G E L E B E E D A P S
E L B U G S P R A Y N G I E A
S I A H G C I C N N M E R C N
C W N L A F I R S K O O B F K
M T A E M I L E L H M R W L J
T A P R E A O R E S L B A A B
S M P A S R R T E N T L U S C
C E A I I R C G P E I U J H A
S S N A C K S S I M O K I L R
I J R S F O I S N J R A Q I D
C Y E T L E V E G U O R V G S
E W T A K C A B B S S O H H M
X J N F I R S T A I D K I T T
U A A E S S E N G E T P V A B
C J L I A R T D N A M A H A S
```

68

# All in the Day of a Park Ranger

There are many right answers for this activity, but not all of the provided examples are good activities for a park ranger. In fact, a park ranger's job may include stopping visitors from doing some of these things.

**The list below are activities that rangers do not do:**

feed the migratory birds

throw rocks off the side of the canyon

pick wildflowers

share marshmallows with squirrels

catch salamanders and make them race

## Answers: National Park Names

ERRIV
(R) I V E R

CETERYME
(C) E M E T E R Y

SHSEAREO
S (E) (A) S H O R E

ESERVER
R (E) S E R V E

ARWAYPK
P A R K W (A) Y

MRIAEMOL
M (E) M O R I A L

RELASHOKE
L A K E S H (O) R E

Now arrange the circled letters to solve one last type of NPS unit.

(R) E (C) R (E) A T I (O) N   A R E (A)

# Answers: Other National Parks Crossword

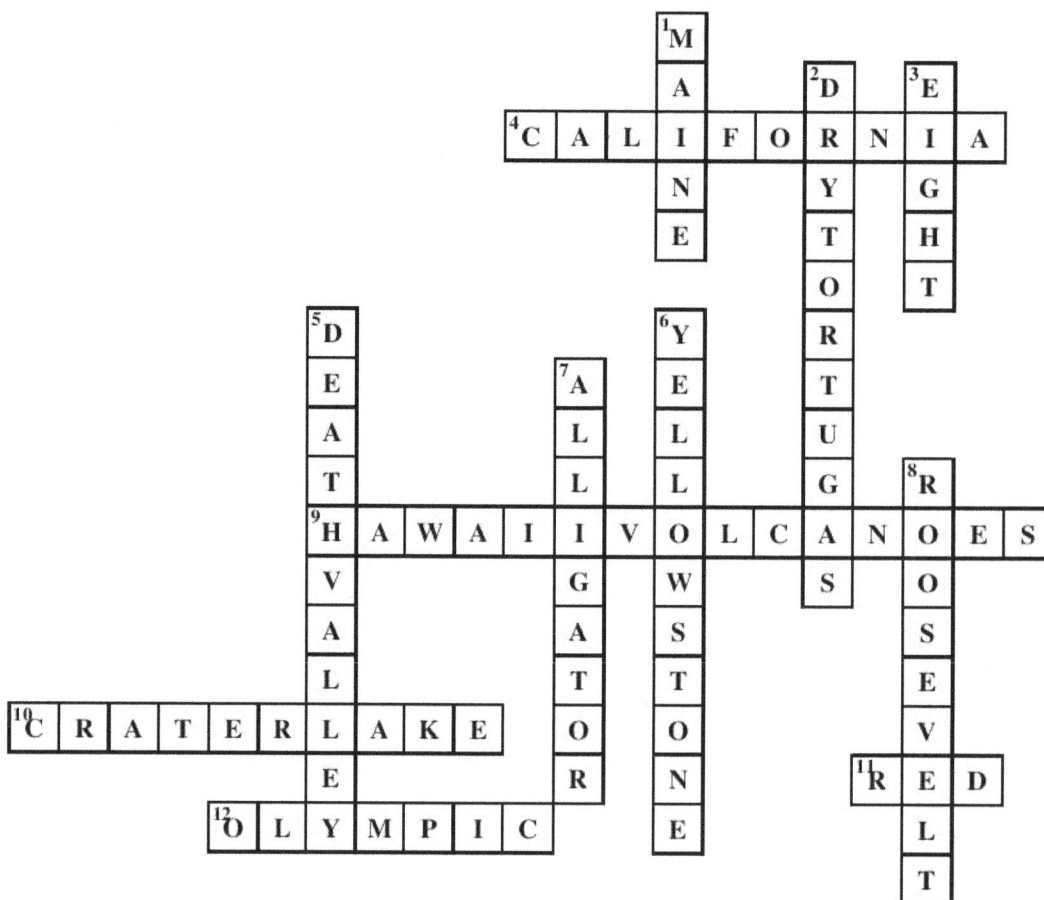

The crossword grid (answers filled in):

Across:
- 4. CALIFORNIA
- 9. HAWAIIVOLCANOES
- 10. CRATERLAKE
- 11. RED
- 12. OLYMPIC

Down:
- 1. MAINE
- 2. DRYTORTUGAS
- 3. EIGHT
- 5. DEATHVALLEY
- 6. YELLOWSTONE
- 7. ALLIGATOR
- 8. ROOSEVELT

## Down

1. State where Acadia National Park is located
2. This National Park has the Spanish word for turtle in it
3. Number of National Parks in Alaska
5. This National Park has some of the hottest temperatures in the world
6. This National Park is the only one in Idaho
7. This toothsome creature can famously be found in Everglades National Park
8. Only president with a national park named for them

## Across

4. This state has the most National Parks
9. This park has some of the newest land in the US, caused by a volcanic eruption
10. This park has the deepest lake in the United States
11. This color shows up in the name of a National Park in California
12. This National Park deserves a gold medal

# Answers: Which National Park Will You Go To Next?

1. Zion
2. Big Bend
3. Glacier
4. Olympic
5. Sequoia
6. Bryce
7. Mesa Verde
8. Biscayne
9. Wind Cave
10. Great Basin
11. Katmai
12. Yellowstone
13. Voyageurs
14. Arches
15. Badlands
16. Denali
17. Glacier Bay
18. Hot Springs

```
F M M E S A V E R D E B N E Y
E A B I G B E N D E S A S E M
Y L I C A L O Y N E E D L T G
D M G A S S A U C N R L U E R
C E L I I T S C R E O A A K E
S N A W Y E E O I W T N A C A
G I C H A A Q C S E M D N S T
N O I Z P R U T I M R S N E B
I W E L M P O N B W E B K H A
R J R F D N I F L I H B U C S
P A B E E S A N E S O P W R I
S J A E N Y A C S I B A U A N
T C Y I A D O H H Y M E A L R
O T A T L M L E S E G R W R J
H S T O I K A T M A I R O P B
I C H U R C O L Y M P I C O U
O Y G T S D E O S B R Y C E T
W I N D C A V E I N R O H E M
```